FOOTBALL BIOGRAPHIES BIBLE FOR KIDS

The Most Complete & Accurate Collection
of Inspiring Stories from Some of the
Best NFL Players of All Time

ROBERT A. MALONE

TABLE OF CONTENTS

INTRODUCTION

Football is one of the most popular sports in the world. It is exciting, fast-paced, and action-packed, offering something for everyone to enjoy. Kids can learn important skills such as teamwork, strategy, communication, discipline, and perseverance from this sport. Football can also help children develop a stronger bond with their teammates, boost their self-confidence, and provide constructive ways to express their creativity. At the same time, football provides an opportunity for physical activity and exercise, allowing kids to stay active and develop healthy habits. It is a great way to not just stay fit but to have fun while doing so. Additionally, it helps ensure that kids get to experience the thrill of victory and the importance of putting in hard work.

Football is a sport that brings people together from all walks of life. It provides an opportunity for people to learn from each other and form lasting friendships. The world of football has given us plenty of stories to share and inspiring players to aspire to. Football offers a great way to bond with family and friends. It is one sport that brings joy and excitement to both kids and adults. It is fun. It is rewarding. But, most importantly, it teaches us a lot about how to attain success in life.

A BRIEF HISTORY OF FOOTBALL

Football has been thrilling audiences of all age groups since its introduction in 1869. It was created by combining two British sports that had become wildly popular in the United States at the time: rugby and soccer. The first official game of football was played between Rutgers and Princeton University in New Jersey, with the former registering a 6-4 victory over the latter. Since then, football has become an integral part of the American culture with countless professional and amateur teams competing in leagues all over the country.

Football is a fun and exciting sport for kids of all ages. It is fast-paced and full of action, with teams competing to outsmart each other on the field. Professional athletes like Jim Brown, Joe Montana, and Walter Payton have made history by becoming some of the greatest players ever in the NFL and CFL, while college teams such as the Texas Longhorns, Ohio State Buckeyes, and Alabama Crimson Tide reign as some of the most successful programs in the country. With ever-changing rules and strategies, the game of football never ceases to be thrilling and unpredictable. Kids of all ages can enjoy participating in youth football leagues or simply watching the game on TV with friends and family. Football is also a great way to make new friends, whether online or on the field. Fans come together to celebrate the highs and lows of the game and share their love for it with others.

From the roar of the stadium crowds to the online community cheering on their favorite teams and players, football has created an environment that celebrates the very best of sportsmanship. Football fans everywhere can come together to root for their favorite teams and share their love for the game. With each passing week, there's a chance to see an epic rivalry begin, promising, new stars emerge, and new records smash old ones - making sure that no two seasons are ever quite the same. In addition to all the fun, football provides an opportunity to learn about sportsmanship, strategy, and teamwork, making it the perfect sport for kids of a formative age.

FOOTBALL BIOGRAPHY FOR KIDS

The Football Biography for Kids offers an in-depth look at the history and evolution of the sport, highlighting the career of some of its most iconic players, their rise to fame, and their greatest moments on the field. In addition, this book dives into stories of hard work, dedication, and success within the football world, providing readers with a unique insight into the inspiring journeys of ten of the sport's greatest stars. With each profile, readers will get to know about the players' early lives, their high school and college experiences, and their rise to fame.

By delving into the fascinating lives of these football icons, this book provides an inspiring glimpse of the sport. It is sure to leave readers with a profound appreciation for the sport and a nuanced understanding of what it takes to get to the top. Whether you're an avid football fan or just enjoy reading inspiring stories, this football biography will make for a great read. It's an entertaining and educational journey through the history of football, making it the perfect companion for young readers looking to learn more about the game.

This meticulously compiled collection of biographical stories not only provides an overview of the players' lives and accomplishments but also dives deep into the unique personalities and stories of each player. Readers will get to experience these players in their own words, as well as gain an understanding of the hard work and dedication it takes to make it to the top. From details on their dreams and motivation to stories of adversity and triumph, this football biography paints a vivid and inspiring picture of the game and its biggest stars.

With the added bonus of interactive quizzes and facts in the book, kids can have fun while absorbing all the information they need to become better-informed football fans.

Not only does this book offer informative facts and figures, but it also provides an emotional connection to some of the biggest stars in football. Through their inspiring stories, readers will learn valuable lessons in perseverance, hard work, and dedication - essential values that make way for success in all aspects of life. So grab your favorite snack and settle in for a memorable journey through football history with this incredibly informative little biography!

CHAPTER ONE: BARRY SANDERS

EARLY LIFE

Barry Sanders is a legendary football player and is widely considered to be one of the greatest running backs of all time. He was born on July 16, 1968, in Wichita, Kansas, and was raised in a large family with four siblings. Whenever he speaks about his siblings, he always mentions the role they played in helping him reach the pinnacle of success. He talks about how they were there to support him all the way and ensure that he never felt lost or alone along the way. Growing up, Sanders was an avid sports fan and was particularly drawn to football.

HIGH SCHOOL

For most athletes, the foundation of their career is usually built in high school, and Sanders was no different. In high school, Sanders proved to be exceptionally gifted in both football and basketball, and quickly became a favorite among students and teachers alike. He was named All-State in both sports and was the team captain of the football team. He was also the team MVP and was known for his leadership on the field. He was extremely hard-working and many claim that he spent hours every day in the gym. Like most other players who made a name for themselves in the world of sports, Sanders started making history right from the beginning. He became the first player in his school to rush for over 1,000 yards in a single season, a truly remarkable feat for a player that young.

Sanders would go on to make and break many more records. Apart from the 1k yard-rush, he was also the first player in school history to be selected to the All-State team in both football and basketball. What made Sanders stand out at such a young age was his strong work ethic and unwavering dedication to the game. He was often seen staying after practice to work on his technique and was known for motivating others in the locker room. His teammates loved him for the constant push he always gave them to be the best.

The greatest people are those who exhibit strength of character, and Sanders distinguished himself with his integrity and humility. He was known for his modesty and willingness to help his teammates. Sanders's glittering high school career paved the way for his success at the collegiate and professional levels. His hard work and dedication to the game of football helped him become one of the greatest running backs of all time.

COLLEGE FOOTBALL CAREER

Sanders continued his stellar performance in college. He attended the Oklahoma State University, where he continued to excel in both football and basketball. During his college career, he was a two-time All-American and won the Heisman Trophy in 1988, enhancing his already impressive portfolio. In time, he became the first player in NCAA history to rush for over 2,000 yards in a single season. All too often, players get injured playing in the rough terrain of college football and are forced to bow out of the sport. Sanders was lucky enough to have made it through college without suffering any major setback. He did sustain a minor ankle injury in his senior year but he didn't let it get in his way. He overcame the injury and went on to lead his team to win the All-American for a second time.

PROFESSIONAL FOOTBALL CAREER

Once a player has been able to successfully play at the collegiate level, the next step on the ladder to success is getting drafted. It marks the beginning of their professional career and offers them the opportunity to play in the big leagues and showcase their talent to the world. Only the very best manage to excel at this level. After college, Sanders got drafted by the Detroit Lions in the 1989 NFL Draft. This was his launch pad to stardom and he knew better than anyone else that only consistently good performance could help him scale the heights that he wanted to scale.

During his professional career, he was a four-time All-Pro and a ten-time Pro Bowl selection. He also went on to win the NFL's Offensive Player of the Year in 1997 and was named the NFL's Most Valuable Player in 1997— remarkable feats for a Kansas boy of humble beginnings. Records are meant to be broken and Sanders smashed quite a few during his time on the field. He, in fact, made the record for the most rushing yards in a single season, with 2,053 yards in 1997, a feat only a select few have been able to match up to. He quickly became a household name, and apart from a minor run-in with the police on account of speeding, for which he was let off with just a warning, he had no other controversies.

When it comes to injuries, Sanders did suffer a few setbacks. In 1999, he tore his ACL which automatically ruled him out of the season and kept him out of the game for an extended period of time. The year 2001 saw him out of the team regularly owing to a persistent back injury. But, in spite of these injuries, Sanders went on to achieve so much more than one would have expected. He was truly one of the greatest players to have ever played the game. He came up with a signature “high-step” running style which helped him avoid being tackled by opponents. So effective was the style that it quickly became popular among other players who tried to copy Sanders as a way to avoid tackles. He was also known for his signature "stutter-step" move, which was a move he would use to make defenders miss.

Sanders’s affable personality and strong bond with his teammates and coaches made him extremely popular among both team members and the general public. Despite being in the public eye for so many years, Sanders managed to make it through his career without any scandal to take the sheen off his impressive career. In 2002, at the end of his illustrious career, Sanders married Lauren Campbell, a news anchor. The couple went on to have three children together.

OFF THE FIELD

When Sanders wasn’t playing, he spent most of his time doing charitable work and helping people within the community. He was a member of the Detroit Lions' Community Outreach Program and was involved with a number of charitable organizations. He was also an avid golfer and enjoyed playing the game in his spare time. Additionally, Sanders became known for his kindness, humility, and generosity. He was often seen signing autographs and interacting with fans and made sure to leave everyone that met him with a smile on their face. His philanthropic activities played a key role in uplifting the underprivileged sections of Kansas, as he donated to a number of charities and causes that advocated for the less privileged.

POST-CAREER

After retiring from the NFL in 1999, Sanders remained involved with football. He was a commentator for ESPN's Sunday NFL Countdown and was a member of the Pro Football Hall of Fame Selection Committee. He also served as an ambassador for the NFL and was a spokesman for Nike. Sanders's legacy is one of greatness, and the several accolades he earned will continue to shine on his successful career.

In an interesting interview with ESPN in 2017, Sanders discussed his career and the legacy he will leave behind. He said, "I'm proud of the way I played the game and the way I represented the game. I hope that I was able to inspire people to work hard and to never give up. I'm proud of the way I was able to play the game and the way I was able to make a difference in the lives of others."

In the same interview, Sanders also discussed his signature "high-step" running style. He said, "I think it was just something I developed over time. I was always trying to find ways to make defenders miss and I think the high-step was something that worked for me. I was able to make defenders miss and it was something that I was able to use to my advantage."

LEGACY

Sanders is known for his incredible athleticism and his ability to make defenders miss. Throughout his career, he distinguished himself with his incredible speed and agility. He was able to make defenders miss with his quickness and was able to break tackles with his strength, which made him one of the most exciting players to watch.

Widely considered one of the greatest running backs of all time, his records and awards speak to his greatness. He was known for his hard work and dedication to the game of football. In 2004, he was inducted into the Pro Football Hall of Fame and his number 20 jersey was retired by the Detroit Lions in 2017. He was also named to the NFL's 100th Anniversary All-Time Team in 2019.

He will also be remembered for his humility and charitable work off the field. Ever modest about his achievements, he rarely boasted about all he had accomplished. He was a leader both on and off the field, and will always be remembered for the lives he touched and the people he uplifted both on and off the field.

CHAPTER TWO: BRETT FAVRE

EARLY CHILDHOOD

Brett Favre was born in Gulfport, Mississippi on October 10, 1969. He was the second of four children born to Irvin and Bonita Favre. Growing up in a small town, Brett was exposed to the game of football at an early age. His father was a high school football coach, and Brett was often seen at practices and games.

He also played baseball and basketball. However, it was football that truly captured his heart.

Brett was always fiercely competitive. His competitive nature revealed itself from an early age. He was known to challenge his older brother, Scott, to arm wrestling matches, and was always up for a game of catch. He was a prankster and loved playing pranks on his siblings and friends.

He was a big fan of the Green Bay Packers, and would often watch their games on TV with his dad. Brett was an avid reader in his youth, and he enjoyed reading books on a variety of topics, including history, philosophy, and sports. He was also an active member of his church and often volunteered to help those in need. His strong faith would become an important part of his life and career.

HIGH SCHOOL

In high school, Brett was a standout athlete, playing quarterback and safety for Hancock North Central High School. He was an all-state selection in both football and baseball. He led his team to the state championship game in 1987, but they were defeated by a score of 14-7. Despite the loss, Brett was named the Mississippi Player of the Year that season.

Brett was also known for his leadership skills and was often seen motivating his teammates and encouraging them to work hard. His competitive streak continued in high school and he often challenged his teammates to arm wrestling matches. He was known for his sense of humor and helped keep the mood light in the locker room with his jokes and pranks.

Brett was a talented quarterback in high school and set numerous school records. He was known for his strong arm and ability to make plays with his feet. He was a good student and was known for helping his teammates with their studies. In addition to being an outstanding athlete, he also distinguished himself as a musician in high school. He also loved hunting and fishing and often spent his weekends in the great outdoors with his family. His exceptional performance both on and off the field made it clear that he was destined for greatness.

Brett experienced his first major setback in high school when he suffered a knee injury during his senior year. He was forced to miss the remainder of the season. However, his determination ensured that he made a full recovery in time for college. He worked hard in physical therapy and got back on his feet in no time. This injury would prove to be only a minor setback in the long run, as he would go on to have a successful college and professional career.

COLLEGE FOOTBALL CAREER

Brett Favre had a successful college career at the University of Southern Mississippi. He was a four-year starter at quarterback and was named to the All-American team in his senior year. During his time at Southern Miss, Favre set numerous school records, including the most touchdown passes in a single season (34) and the most career touchdown passes (57). He also led the Golden Eagles to three consecutive bowl appearances, including the 1988 Independence Bowl. Favre was a two-time winner of the Conerly Trophy, which is awarded to the best college football player in Mississippi. He was also named the MVP of the 1990 Senior Bowl and was selected to the All-South Independent Team in 1989 and 1990.

Favre earned a reputation for his strength and resilience. He gave his 100% in each game even while battling serious injuries. He was also known for his leadership skills and inspiring speeches - so much so that he was voted the most motivational player on the team in his senior year. While he did sustain a few unfortunate setbacks in college, including a knee injury and drunk-driving suspension, Favre managed to bounce back and have a successful career.

Favre's college career, in fact, turned out to be a stupendous success, marked by a Hail Mary pass to beat Tulane in 1989, and a game-winning touchdown pass against Alabama the following year. The future NFL great became known for his infectious enthusiasm and passion for the game, and his bond with his offensive line proved invaluable. He was also a promising golfer and a member of the school's golf team. His outgoing personality made him very popular at social events. Favre was quite the social butterfly during his time at Southern Miss, as a member of the Sigma Alpha Epsilon fraternity, and is still remembered fondly by the Southern Miss community. He was a leader on and off the field and a great example of what it takes to be successful in football. It's no wonder then that his college career would be a springboard for an even more successful NFL career.

PROFESSIONAL CAREER

Brett Favre's career was second to none. Brett Favre was drafted by the Falcons in 1991 and won Offensive Rookie of the Year. He was then traded to the Green Bay Packers, with whom he went on to have an incredibly successful stint. He won many accolades including three MVP awards, 11 Pro Bowl selections, the NFL's All-Decade Team of the 90s, a Super Bowl win in 1997, and multiple passing records. His enthusiasm and passion for the game made him an icon both on and off the field, and his leadership skills set a new example in the sport. He left a mark on the NFL that not even time can efface.

Brett Favre wasn't merely a member of some of the greatest teams in NFL history. He led most of these teams to their most memorable victories. He took the Green Bay Packers to a Super Bowl victory in 1997 and a run of four consecutive NFC Championship appearances between 1995 and 1998. His leadership skills were further demonstrated during his stint with the Minnesota Vikings as he led them to the NFC Championship game in 2009. Even during his rookie season with the Atlanta Falcons, he took them all the way to the playoffs in 1991. Favre was a master of his craft, with three MVP awards, 11 Pro Bowl selections, and a 2016 Hall of Fame induction. Despite a nagging injury in his shoulder and his battle with substance abuse, he managed to scale great highs until his retirement in 2010. He, in fact, helped create one of the most iconic moments in NFL history when he threw a miraculous game-winning touchdown pass to Andre Rison in the final seconds of the NFC Championship game against the Dallas Cowboys in 2015.

Favre made history in the 1995 NFC Championship game, famously known as "The Heidi Game”. When he returned to Lambeau Field as a member of the Minnesota Vikings in 2009, the crowd erupted in cheers, honoring his immense contributions to the team and the game of football and highlighting his influence over generations of football fans. He is an inspiration to many, and his legacy will live on for years to come.

OFF THE FIELD

Brett Favre is not only an NFL legend but also a philanthropist who uses his fame to support causes like the Make-A-Wish Foundation and the Boys & Girls Club of America. When he's off the field, Favre enjoys hunting, fishing, golfing, cards, and of course, watching football. He's been happily married to Deanna Tynes since 1996, and they have two beautiful daughters, Brittany, and Breleigh. Favre has been featured in a lot of popular media outlets like ESPN and Sports.

Favre’s career, however, has not been without controversies. In 2010, he was accused of sending inappropriate text messages to a former New York Jets employee. He was also accused of taking painkillers without a prescription during his time with the Jets. More recently, in 2015, Favre was again cited for allegedly sending inappropriate messages to a female reporter. Despite this, Favre remains an icon and continues to be applauded for his involvement in charitable causes.

POST CAREER

After retiring from the NFL in 2010, Favre stayed connected to the game he loves by coaching high school football teams and making a brief return to the NFL in 2012. He's also been involved in several business ventures, including opening a restaurant and launching a steak sauce. Favre also supports an array of charitable causes and organizations, like the Brett Favre Fourward Foundation, which helps underprivileged children. In 2016, he was inducted into the Pro Football Hall of Fame, with over 50,000 people in attendance, and a special documentary "Brett Favre: A Football Life" aired on NFL Network.

After his retirement, Favre has remained in the public eye by frequently appearing as a guest on various talk shows, such as The Tonight Show with Jimmy Fallon and The Ellen DeGeneres Show. He's also been featured in several commercials, including one for Snickers. Overall, Brett Favre's career after football has been a tremendous success. His multiple business ventures have been quite successful and his charitable work has only bolstered his fame.

LEGACY

Brett Favre will forever be remembered for his incredible feats on the football field. His consecutive starts streak, heroic game-winning touchdown pass against the Oakland Raiders, and emotional retirement speech will never be forgotten. He's also known for his famous quote, "It's time to move on and restart my life again," which has become an inspiration to many. His legacy lives on through his awards, records, and quotes.

CHAPTER THREE: CALVIN JOHNSON

EARLY LIFE AND CHILDHOOD

Calvin Johnson, famously known as "Megatron", was born and raised in Newnan, Georgia. He grew up in a large family with four siblings. Johnson's father, Calvin Sr., was an avid athlete who inspired his son to strive for greatness and take the sport of football seriously. Johnson joined the local Pop Warner football team at the age of eight and quickly made a name for himself with his impressive size, strength, and speed. Throughout his early football career, Johnson worked hard to improve and reach his goals. His dedication and perseverance helped him attain success very quickly. He was given special recognition from his high school Sandy Creek High as well as the Georgia Sports Writers Association. Johnson used these early successes as a stepping stone toward his future NFL career.

As a child, Calvin was well known in the local Newnan area for his athletic prowess. He often won awards and recognition for his performance in sports and quickly developed into a star player in both football and basketball. He did suffer a few setbacks, such as being cut from a few of his youth football teams due to his size. Yet, this did not deter Calvin and he continued to work hard and strive for success. His hard work and dedication would go on to pay off in the long run and he eventually became one of the best wide receivers in the NFL.

HIGH SCHOOL

Calvin Johnson's high school career was marked by great success. He earned All-State honors in both football and basketball and led Sandy Creek High School to two state championships. In football, he became the first sophomore ever to start for the team and set school records for most receptions and receiving yards in a season. He also earned numerous awards and accolades, including being named to the Georgia Sports Hall of Fame's "Class of 2006". Calvin did suffer from several minor injuries, especially in his shoulder and ankle, which forced him to sit out some games. But he quickly recovered from these injuries and continued his good streak.

While at Sandy Creek, Calvin also made sure to give back to his community. He regularly attended local elementary schools to speak with children and promote the importance of education. He also volunteered with several local charities, such as the Boys & Girls Club and the Special Olympics. Additionally, he was a leader in his school's Fellowship of Christian Athletes group and worked to promote faith in the school and community. His selflessness and dedication to improving the lives of those around him made him a very popular person.

Calvin Johnson was an amazing leader both on and off the field. Not only did he break records and lead his team to two state championships, but he also stayed after practices to mentor younger players and motivate them to reach their full potential. His influence extended beyond the football field and into the community where he served as an example of hard work and dedication. He was also a dedicated student who took his studies seriously, thus, becoming a perfect role model for youngsters. Calvin strived to excel in the classroom and was able to maintain a 3.7 GPA during his senior year. He was also actively involved in extracurricular activities such as the National Honor Society and served as a student representative on several school committees. Overall, Calvin Johnson performed exceptionally well in school, demonstrating that hard work and dedication can lead to lasting success.

COLLEGE FOOTBALL CAREER

Calvin Johnson's remarkable NFL career was preceded by an equally impressive college football career. A two-time All-American, Johnson played for the Georgia Tech Yellow Jackets from 2004 to 2006. During his three seasons as a wide receiver for the Yellow Jackets, Johnson made an incredible impact with 109 receptions for 1,873 yards and fifteen touchdowns. On the field, Johnson's athletic ability was on full display. His combination of speed and size, along with his great hands, made him a nightmare for opposing defenses. In addition to dominating in the passing game, Johnson also made an impact as a kick returner, averaging nearly 27 yards per return.

He was even a part of the kick return team that set the NCAA record for average yards per game. Off the field, Johnson had a great attitude and was a leader for his team. He was named team captain his senior year, demonstrating his dedication and commitment to the Yellow Jackets. His work ethic also earned him the Bobby Dodd Award as well as the ACC Player of the Year in 2006. During his college career at Georgia Tech, Calvin Johnson suffered multiple injuries which set him back. During his freshman season, he missed four games with a hamstring injury, and then later on in his career, he sustained another hamstring injury which forced him to miss the 2007 Gator Bowl. Despite these setbacks, Johnson was still able to make a great impact on the Yellow Jackets and go on to have a successful career in the NFL. Despite facing criticism from teammates and coaches, Calvin Johnson persevered and worked hard to prove his worth. He eventually earned himself the honors of team captain and ACC Player of the Year his senior season - a true testament to his dedication and hard work!

PROFESSIONAL CAREER

After completing his college career at Georgia Tech, Calvin Johnson was drafted second overall by the Detroit Lions in the 2007 NFL draft. Johnson was expected to make an immediate impact, but a few early injuries caused him to miss some time on the field. Despite this initial setback, Johnson went on to have an illustrious career in the NFL, earning the nickname 'Megatron' for his explosive plays and becoming one of the most dominant wide receivers in the league. He set several records, including becoming the first player in the NFL to have consecutive seasons of 1,600 yards or more receiving. Throughout his time in Detroit, Johnson received great recognition for his stellar play. His accolades include six Pro Bowl selections and being named an All-Pro three times. He also broke an NFL record with 329 receiving yards in a single game and even set the Lions' franchise record for receptions, receiving yards, and touchdowns.

In addition to his on-field success, Johnson's work ethic and attitude earned him the respect of both his teammates and coaches. Throughout his time in Detroit, he distinguished himself as a leader and mentor by putting the interests of his team first and working extra hard to make sure the Lions succeeded. Johnson went on to finish his career on a high note and continues to be celebrated for his determination and resilience.

OFF THE FIELD

Off the field, Johnson was a unifying presence in and around Detroit. He enjoyed giving back to his community, often dedicating his time to charities and making appearances at local schools. Johnson also had an interest in music and art, and even had a passion for cooking. While he may not be as well-known publicly as some of his contemporaries, Johnson did receive plenty of media coverage throughout his career. He did get embroiled in a few controversies. There was a civil lawsuit against him for defamation of character and he was also heavily criticized for an alleged obscene gesture. However, the obscene gesture turned out to be merely a misunderstanding, and the lawsuit against him was also eventually dismissed.

POST CAREER

After retiring from the NFL in 2017, Calvin Johnson has pursued several other equally successful ventures. He has made appearances on multiple radio and TV shows, and has also embarked on a business venture with his brother to create a sports apparel line. In addition to his business endeavors, Johnson has been actively involved with many charity organizations. He even founded the "Calvin Johnson Jr. Foundation" which helps provide educational opportunities for Detroit's youth. Johnson's philanthropy and various business projects have made him a highly sought-after speaker and he has continued to receive positive media coverage throughout his post-career. He continues to remain a source of inspiration for many young players who wish to follow in his footsteps.

LEGACY

Due to his successful NFL career, Calvin Johnson has left a lasting impression on the game of football. Not only did he set numerous records, but he also earned multiple awards during his time in Detroit. He was selected for six Pro Bowls, was named an All Pro three times and even set the Lions franchise record for receptions, receiving yards, and touchdowns. The impact he had on the game is not only remembered through his individual accolades but also through the impact he had on his teammates and coaches. His work ethic and leadership inspired those around him and his 'never give up' attitude will be remembered by many. The phrases used to describe him such as the "Megatron" and "The Catch" are still widely used by football fans. His legacy will, no doubt, stand the test of time.

CHAPTER FOUR: DAN MARINO

EARLY LIFE

Dan Marino was born in Pittsburgh, Pennsylvania and raised in Oakland, a small town located south of the city. He was the youngest of five siblings. He had an older brother who was also an accomplished athlete. Growing up in a family of athletes, Dan was naturally drawn to sports. He developed a passion for football at an early age and quickly gained recognition for his skill and drive for the game.

By the age of eight, Marino had already begun playing organized football and by thirteen he had started playing as the quarterback in his high school football team. He displayed great promise on the field from an early age and, during his time in high school, Dan was named MVP of the 1984 Big 33 Football Classic.

Growing up, Marino was known for his dedication and hard work. His parents emphasized the importance of education and encouraged him to get good grades in school. He also began to lift weights and work on his football skills regularly. During high school, he worked part-time jobs such as delivering newspapers and doing yard work to help support his family.

HIGH SCHOOL CAREER

Dan Marino is one of the biggest names to come out of the high school football scene. He attended Central Catholic High School in Pittsburgh, Pennsylvania and immediately made a mark with his incredible talent. As a freshman, he was already starting as a varsity quarterback and captivated the crowds with his precise passing and decision-making abilities. Throughout his high school career, Marino showed his potential as one of the team's best prospects, helping lead Central Catholic to two Pennsylvania high school championships. In his senior year, Marino won the Pittsburgh City Player of the Year award and was named Parade All-American. Furthermore, he was selected to play in the Big 33 All-Star Football Classic, which pits the best high school players against one another.

Marino was also a strong contender for the Heisman Trophy during his senior year and missed out on the honor narrowly. Despite this, it became very clear to everyone following his career that an incredibly bright future awaited him. Off the field, Marino was known for being a hard worker and respected leader, often staying late after practice to help his teammates better understand the playbook and options on the field. This level of determination and commitment to excellence set him apart from everyone else, and he is still remembered fondly by those at Central Catholic High School.

During his senior year, he won the Pittsburgh City Player of the Year award and was selected to play in the Big 33 All-Star Football Classic. But when the time came to participate in the game, Marino's eligibility was suddenly in question. He had failed a math course, which threatened to prevent him from playing in the classic. Fortunately, a friend of his stepped in and got him the extra credit that he needed to pass the course just in time for the big game.

COLLEGE FOOTBALL CAREER

Dan Marino found great success at the college level, playing for the University of Pittsburgh between 1979 and 1982. During this period, he became one of the most decorated quarterbacks in the school's history, breaking numerous records and setting new standards for excellence. In his freshman year, he was already being touted as a Heisman Trophy candidate and led the team to a couple of successful seasons. He also won numerous awards during his college career, including the Walter Camp Award as the nation's top player and the Maxwell Award, which is annually presented to the best collegiate football player. Marino's leadership played a key role in his team's success. He played with poise and confidence and helped his team make a deep run in the 1981 NCAA playoffs. Despite losing to the University of Georgia, Marino firmly established himself as one of the top quarterbacks in the nation.

Aside from his many successes on the field, Marino was also known for being a hard worker and a great teammate. He was often seen helping and guiding his younger teammates. His dedication and commitment to excellence shone throughout his professional career. Even today, Dan Marino is widely respected for being one of the best QBs in college football history. His ability to lead a team and make remarkable plays despite setbacks and injuries is something that will always remain an example for others to follow.

While Dan Marino rarely experienced any major injury during his college days, he did suffer from a nagging ankle injury during his senior season. This eventually led to him sitting out the last four games of the regular season, thereby ending his hopes of winning the Heisman Trophy that year. But, despite this injury, Marino's resilience still shone through as he was able to make a full recovery and complete his final season on a high note.

PROFESSIONAL CAREER

Dan Marino's professional career began when he was drafted by the Miami Dolphins in 1983. He made his presence felt immediately and went on to become one of the best quarterbacks in NFL history. Over the next 17 years, he would lead the Dolphins to numerous playoff appearances and throw for over 61,000 yards and 420 touchdowns. During this time, Marino was also able to win multiple awards, including numerous Pro Bowl selections and being named the NFL MVP in 1984. He also threw for a record-setting 5,084 yards in 1984 and set a new single-season record for touchdown passes with 48 in 1986.

In 1992, Marino sustained the first major injury of his professional career. He suffered an Achilles tendon tear during a preseason game, which forced him to miss the entire season. This injury threatened to halt Marino's strong run but he managed to bounce back. Dan Marino's professional career was simply extraordinary. From the moment he was drafted by the Miami Dolphins in 1983 until his retirement in 2000, he showed remarkable skill, poise, and leadership — qualities that would go on to make him one of the greatest quarterbacks of all time. He helped lead the team to numerous playoff appearances over the years and set various records for passing yards and touchdown passes. His determination and commitment to excellence showed in the way he pushed through any injury or setback that came his way. This resilience earned him a lot of respect, making him an inspirational figure to many football fans.

Dan Marino almost signed with the Oakland Raiders, but ultimately chose to go with the Miami Dolphins after a call from then-coach Don Shula. This decision marked a big turning point in his career and paved the way for one of the most successful eras in Dolphins' history, culminating in his eventual induction into the Hall of Fame. Despite all the other offers, he went with the Dolphins and pushed through all obstacles to prove his detractors wrong.

OFF THE FIELD

Dan Marino was just as remarkable in his personal life as he was on the football field. As a philanthropist, he founded the Dan Marino Foundation to help children with developmental disabilities. He was involved with several other charitable activities, including the Make-A-Wish Foundation and the United Way. He earned a lot of respect for his generous spirit and commitment to helping others. He had a wide range of interests and hobbies, from golf and seafood to Italian culture and music. His close relationship with the Miami Dolphins continued even after his retirement, as he remained involved with the organization in various capacities. Marino's media presence was quite strong. He appeared in many TV shows and commercials, and even co-starred in a movie titled “Ace Ventura: Pet Detective” alongside Jim Carrey.

The "Muddgate" scandal made a serious dent in his reputation. It was arguably the most infamous episode of his career. The controversy surrounded the hiring of a new coach and Marino was accused of leaking team secrets to the press. This eventually led to him being fined by the team. He even received death threats from fans. Although he was eventually cleared of any wrongdoing, the incident left a dark stain on his legacy. "Muddgate", nonetheless, serves as a reminder of Marino's strength and resilience as, when faced with adversity, the former footballer went to great lengths to protect himself and his team.

POST CAREER

After his retirement, Dan Marino became a prominent figure in the sports media industry and a regular fixture in NFL coverage. He went on to become a studio analyst on the NFL Today show, a consultant for the Miami Dolphins, and an ambassador for the Super Bowl.

Marino has also made an immense contribution to various charities and donated generously to his alma mater, the University of Pittsburgh. Marino successfully welded his deep concern for the community with profitable business ventures. He created Marino Capital and Dan Marino Foundation, both of which focus on helping disadvantaged children. He also served as a partner of H.I.G. Capital and formed the Dan Marino Group to invest in business opportunities that could benefit the local community. Dan Marino's post-career story is an inspiring one. From receiving multiple honors and accolades to helming successful business ventures and making contributions to charity and media, his legacy remains unscarred by the "Muddgate" scandal. His story serves as an example of how one person can make a lasting impression in many lives.

LEGACY

The impact that Dan Marino had on the game cannot be described in words. His legacy will live on for years to come. He even had an inspirational quote immortalized: "Always stay focused on what you set out to do and never let anything deter you from achieving it". His passion and hard work will be remembered and relived through the stories and experiences shared by the generations that follow. A truly inspirational figure, his courage, commitment to excellence, and resilience will continue to be an example for future generations to follow.

CHAPTER FIVE: DEION SANDERS

EARLY LIFE AND CHILDHOOD

Deion Sanders was born in the small town of Fort Myers, Florida to Connie Knight and Mims Sanders. His humble beginnings instilled in him the values of perseverance and dedication which helped him hone his innate talent in sports. Deion Sanders has credited much of his drive and determination to his upbringing, and remains very close to his parents and siblings.

He was a gifted athlete from an early age and found success in football, basketball, baseball, and track. In addition to sports, Sanders also had a passion for music. When he was 12 years old, he saw one of his favorite songs performed on The Arsenio Hall Show and decided then and there that he wanted to make his own music. This early dream eventually led to the release of his rap album in 1996.

Deion Sanders experienced several setbacks during his childhood. Most notably, he failed to make the varsity football team in his freshman year at North Fort Myers High School. However, he refused to give up and worked hard to improve his skills. He eventually made the varsity team in his sophomore year and went on to become an All-American defensive back and kick returner. This was one of the early signs of his remarkable perseverance and determination in the face of failure.

HIGH SCHOOL

When Deion Sanders was in high school, he shone in various sports such as football, basketball, baseball, and track. His dedication to attaining the highest level of performance was recognized when he was awarded the Florida Player of the Year, as well as the USA Today Player of the Year. He eventually went on to earn a scholarship to attend Florida State University. However, many of the scouts lost interest in him after he suffered an ankle sprain while playing basketball during his junior year. This caused him to miss a lot of time on the field. He did not, however, give up and put in a lot of effort to rehabilitate his ankle. He became successful eventually and made a full recovery from his injury.

The fact that Deion Sanders was able to succeed throughout his high school career despite so many setbacks speaks to his tremendous willpower and dedication. He muscled through his injury and the scrutiny of scouts to realize his dreams. As a result of his dogged perseverance and indomitable spirit, he was able to win a number of accolades and ultimately a scholarship to attend Florida State University, which served as the launch pad for his extraordinary career.

Deion Sanders had to surmount many challenges during his time as a student in high school, but he never lost sight of the goals he had set for himself. His persistent efforts would go on to make him a role model for a large number of up-and-coming athletes. His story serves as a timely reminder that if one is dedicated and determined, there is no limit to what one can achieve. Even in this day and age, his narrative continues to motivate people and encourage others to persevere in the face of challenges in order to achieve their goals. A model student and athlete in high school, Deion Sanders was the first person in the state of Florida to have his jersey retired after he became the first player to have his number retired.

COLLEGE FOOTBALL CAREER

During his time in college, Deion Sanders established himself as a formidable opponent. At Florida State University, he was a standout on defense and garnered various accolades as a kick returner. He broke a number of school records along the way. In 1987 and 1988, he was recognized as an All-American defensive back by the Associated Press, and in 1988, he was a finalist for the Heisman Trophy. Sanders was also well-known for his unique showy style of play, which consisted of mesmerizing fans as well as opposing teams with his remarkable agility and quickness. The time he spent playing college football was not only packed with memorable accomplishments and anecdotes but also with experiences that were one-of-a-kind, such as the time he blocked three punts in a single game or the time he returned a punt for a score in the same game. While Sanders's time as a college student was marked by success, it also witnessed quite a few setbacks. The most notable among these setbacks was an ankle injury he sustained in 1988 that left him out of the entire season that year, including the Orange Bowl game.

In spite of these challenges, he persisted in pushing himself and aiming for the highest level of performance. The Atlanta Falcons recognized his hard work and dedication and selected him fifth overall in the NFL draft in 1989. That year, he finally received his due recognition. Sanders's undergraduate career is now the stuff of legend and serves as a shining example of what can be achieved with consistent effort and dogged pursuit of one's goals. Since then, he has been inducted into the Pro Football Hall of Fame, further confirming his position as one of the most accomplished athletes in the history of the sport. His academic success at the university serves as a reminder that it is possible to excel in both domains as long as one puts in the effort.

Following his graduation from college, Sanders became the first player in the history of professional sports to have successful careers in both the sport of football and the sport of baseball. Fans were blown away by his ability to excel in both sports, and he was recognized for it with a number of accolades and honors, including the NFL Defensive Player of the Year Award, the NFL Pro Bowl MVP Award, and repeated selection to the All-Pro team. His versatility has led to him being regarded as one of the best athletes in history.

PROFESSIONAL FOOTBALL CAREER

Deion Sanders is certainly one of the greatest figures to ever grace a football field. He has achieved success at every level of his football career, both collegiate and professional. He was the first player to play in a Super Bowl and a World Series and the only athlete to have hit a home run and scored a touchdown in the same week. Deion's excellence on the field has led him to win a number of awards, including eight Pro Bowl selections, two NFL Defensive Player of the Year awards, and a consensus All-American selection during his college days.

Aside from his accomplishments as a professional athlete, Deion also achieved success off the field. He inspired a generation of young fans with his charisma and swagger, earning nicknames such as "Primetime" and "Neon Deion". He was also a pioneer in the business of sports, launching his own record label, becoming an analyst for NFL Network, and eventually becoming an owner in the Arena Football League.

Deion's professional career was beset by a number of injuries much like those he witnessed during his college days. His rookie season was hampered by a severe hamstring injury, and he went on to suffer numerous other physical ailments throughout his playing days. But, Deon always managed to overcome the obstacles that came his way. Deion proved himself to be a true powerhouse in every sense of the word, both on and off the field.

In interviews, Deion said that what made him such a successful athlete was his unyielding confidence, relentless work ethic, and ability to push himself past any obstacle that life put in front of him. He often said that if one wants something bad enough, one will find a way to get it. This mantra served him well throughout his career, and will surely continue to do so far beyond.

OFF THE FIELD

In 2017, Deion Sanders founded the Prime 21 Foundation, which is committed to helping economically challenged student-athletes to achieve their academic and athletic goals. In addition to his charitable endeavors, Deion has also had a lengthy media career. Deion has been married twice and is a father of six children. He often spends his free time with his family, traveling to exotic locations and attending sporting events. He also frequently donates to charitable causes, such as the Boys & Girls Club, as a way to give back to the community. Deion's career has not been without controversies. In 2011, he was accused of owing millions in child support to his ex-wife. Although he eventually settled the case, the dispute brought to light these questionable financial decisions. He is, nonetheless, celebrated for helping those that are in need. Whether it's working on the football field or using his platform to bring awareness to social issues, Deion Sanders continues to be a role model to many.

POST CAREER

After retiring from sports, Deion began a successful media career. He worked as an analyst and commentator for the NFL Network, CBS Sports, and Fox Sports. His signature catchphrases and larger-than-life personality quickly made him a hit on TV. Deion has also been involved in several business ventures since retiring. In 2008, he became the CEO and President of the Leadership Education & Athletics Foundation, which seeks to improve the lives of children through education and sports. He also owns several sports-based businesses and consults with many professional athletes.

LEGACY

Deion Sanders is an iconic figure in NFL history. His prowess on the field made him one of the most exciting players to watch, and his flair for the dramatic has made him one of the most popular players on the field. His charitable work has earned him multiple awards, while his "Must Be The Money" quote has become shorthand to describe elite athletes with extraordinary talent. His lasting legacy has been immortalized in sports films, books and television shows, and his work as an analyst and commentator is highly regarded. He has been an inspiration to many and his impact goes far beyond sports. He is a prime example of how hard work and dedication can lead to great success, both on and off the field. Through his determination, poise, and charisma, he has become an iconic figure in NFL history and his influence will surely be felt for years to come.

CHAPTER SIX: DEACON JONES

In the minds of today's NFL fans, the Pro Football Hall of Fame is where the game's storied past may forever be guarded. Only, the most famous athletes, are allowed into the Hall of Fame, immortalized in bronze and displayed. The entrance is guarded by panels of seasoned journalists and athletes. The black-and-white images and mottled plaques speak of a bygone era and relics of the past that seems as distant as a dream. Deacon Jones, however, is no relic. The frightening blend of strength, speed, and viciousness that made Jones a force to be reckoned with during his professional days continues to be celebrated today. His talent transcends ages and it is very likely that he would have been a first-round pick in this year's draft as well.

When Jones first entered the league, still and moving films were primarily black and white, but his presence on the field was like a burst of full-color, high-definition, 240-frames-per-second animation. Jones came and altered the nature of NFL scoring drives for good. In many ways, he served as an inspiration for modern explosive defensive linemen. Many of the game's greatest pass rushers from different eras and clubs have spoken out in the wake of Jones' death to honor a man who was so profoundly influential to their careers.

EARLY LIFE

Deacon Jones, born David Jones on December 9th, 1938, in Eatonville, Florida, was an American football player in the NFL. From a very young age, he was a sports enthusiast, regularly participating in football, baseball, and basketball. As a teen, he was diagnosed with a tumor in his thigh, and had to undergo surgery to remove it. He also experienced racism as a child. His experiences not only shaped his football career but also inspired him to work for civil rights as an adult. He once saw a car full of youngsters attack an old black woman on her way to church. She later died from her injuries but the incident was never recorded or investigated by authorities. Jones explained years later in an interview that he turned to football, a sport known for its bloody history, primarily to channel the feelings of wrath and frustration he felt after witnessing that woman's tragic end specifically and racial injustice in general.

COLLEGE LIFE

Jones spent the 1958 football season at South Carolina State University, and then sat out 1959 to focus on his studies at Mississippi Valley (then known as Mississippi Vocational College) before graduating in 1960. Legend has it that when the state of South Carolina discovered that Jones participated in a Civil Rights Movement rally, they decided to withdraw his scholarship as a punishment. Luckily for Jones, one of South Carolina State's assistant football coaches was leaving to become the head coach at Mississippi Vocational. He convinced Jones and some of the other black players to join him, assuring them that he could secure them scholarships there. In 1960, Jones secured a place in Mississippi Vocational College on a full scholarship, thanks to the generosity of his coach. Jones's brush with racism did not end here, however. While playing basketball at Mississippi Vocational, he and his African-American teammates were routinely turned away from motels. They had to sleep on cots in the gym of their opponents. His experiences would go on to exert a profound influence on his style of play.

CAREER

Jones went primarily unnoticed during his collegiate career because of the lack of television coverage and the absence of contemporary scouting networks. This is what led author Ray Didinger to tell NFL Films that "it was more or less by chance that Deacon was uncovered. While looking for a new running back, the Rams discovered a defensive tackle who could outrun any of the prospects they had seen so far". Jones was selected by the Los Angeles Rams in the 14th round of the 1961 National Football League draft. After being selected by the Rams, Jones went on to become a starting defensive end for the team. Following his retirement, he would team up with tackle Merlin Olsen to form the Rams' regular All-Pro left defensive line. With Lamar Lundy, Rosey Grier, and Merlin Olsen, he became a member of the Rams' Fearsome Foursome defensive line, widely regarded as one of the best of all time.

Jones was named to the consensus All-Pro team for five consecutive years, from 1965 to 1969, and to the All-Pro second team in 1964, 1970, and 1972. From 1964 to 1970, he played in the Pro Bowl, and following the 1972 season, the San Diego Chargers drafted him to his eighth Pro Bowl. In 1962, 1964, 1965, and 1966, the Los Angeles Rams alumni selected him as the team's Outstanding Defensive Lineman. Jones missed four starts in 1971 because of a badly sprained arch, and he finished the year with 412 sacks, his lowest total ever.

The Rams sent Jones, Lee White, and Greg Wojcik to the Chargers on January 29th, 1972, in exchange for Jeff Staggs, the 30th overall pick in the 1972 second round (Jim Bertelsen), and the 31st and 60th picks in the 1973 second and third rounds (Cullen Bryant and Tim Stokes, respectively).

He led all Chargers defensive linemen in tackles, was chosen defensive captain, and was selected to play for the AFC in the Pro Bowl. In 1974, he retired after playing for the Washington Redskins. The Redskins allowed him to kick the extra point after his final touchdown in his last NFL game. Jones earned four weekly honors as the NFL's Defensive Player of the Week from the Associated Press: in Weeks 14, 12, and 10, respectively, in 1967, 1968, and 1970.

Jones, who played in the NFL for 14 seasons, was only suspended for six games the entire time, missing only six regular season matchups.

SACKS

Many people thought Jones would completely revamp the defensive end role. The term "sacking the quarterback" originated with him. In 1999, Jones gave a Los Angeles Times reporter a description of his specialty: "You take all the offensive linemen and put them in a burlap bag, and then you take a baseball bat and beat on the bag. You're not just putting them in the bag; you're saddling them. That's precisely how you use a quarterback."

Jones's quickness and unique ability to make tackles from sideline to sideline set him apart from every other defensive end of his era. He also pioneered the usage of the head slap by a pass rusher, explaining that he did it "to give myself an initial head start on the pass rush, in other words, an extra stride".He added, "because it's human nature to reflexively close one's eyes or blink when struck on the back of the head, whether by a man or a woman. I mean, that's it, that's it, that's all I needed. I didn't come up with the head slap, but then again, neither did Rembrandt. The quickness of my hands and the length of my arms were perfect for me. It was the greatest thing I ever did, and when I left the game, they outlawed it".

According to Pro Football Weekly, he finished his career with 173 and a half sack, good enough for third place on the all-time sacks list. (Jones would have been first all-time if he hadn't retired; since then, Bruce Smith and Reggie White have joined the Hall of Fame and passed him.)

Jones recorded 21 and a half sacks in just 14 games in 1967 and then 22 sacks in the same number of games the following year. If confirmed, this would have been an NFL record that wouldn't have been broken until Harvey Martin recorded 23 sacks in 1977. Al Baker matched that total a year later. The phrase "sack" wasn't coined until later, and the NFL didn't keep official sack statistics until 1982.

CAREER AFTER FOOTBALL

- **Acting**

Jones had an impressive career in television and made numerous guest appearances on shows during the 1970s and beyond. One episode of "The Odd Couple" featured him in an Oscar commercial for men's shaving supplies. He was a guard in the Giant's castle in the Bewitched episode "Sam & the Beanstalk" from 1969 and also appeared in "The Brady Bunch". In a 1978 episode of "Wonder Woman", Jones appeared as himself. In the 1978 film "The Norseman", he portrayed the role of a Viking named Thall. A second Norseman, played by fellow Hall of Famer Fred Biletnikoff, appeared alongside Jones in the film. That same year, "Heaven Can Wait" was released, where Jones played the role of Gorman, a ferocious defensive lineman.

- **Broadcasting**

During the 1994 season, Jones worked alongside Steve Physioc and Jack Snow as a color analyst for KMPC radio broadcasts of Rams games. When the Denver Broncos faced the Green Bay Packers in Super Bowl XXXII in 1998, Jones correctly predicted the underdog Broncos would win and that Terrell Davis would be voted the game's most valuable player.

- **Business**

In addition to his work for the NFL and Champion Products' Throwback campaigns, Jones modeled for several clothing companies and medical enterprises. He also led the hypertension education initiative for AstraZeneca Pharmaceuticals, which spanned the country.

- **Volunteerism**

According to NFL.com, Jones has made multiple trips to Iraq to meet with American troops. In 1997, Jones established the non-profit Deacon Jones Foundation to provide the youth and their local communities with a holistic program that emphasizes education, mentoring from adult role models, corporate internships, and volunteer work.

- **Restoring the NFL's presence in Southern California**

Jones was among the many former Los Angeles Rams unhappy with the move to St. Louis in 1995. Whenever he was interviewed, he adamantly insisted that he played for the Los Angeles Rams and not the St. Louis Rams. He even went so far as to suggest that the St. Louis Rams should change their name. He participated in many grassroots movements and publicly supported numerous stadium proposals to bring NFL football back to Los Angeles. The Rams eventually relocated back to LA though Jones had passed away by then.

ACHIEVEMENT

After being selected to the NFL's 75th Anniversary All-Time Team in 1994, he was inducted into the Pro Football Hall of Fame in 1980, his first year of eligibility. In 1999, he was rated number thirteen on ESPN's list of the 100 Greatest Football Players. He led all defensive ends in terms of popularity and was second on the list among defensive linemen, behind only Bob Lilly. Earlier that very year, he was dubbed the "Defensive End of the Century" by Sports Illustrated. He entered the Black College Football Hall of Fame with its first class in 2010.

The year 1980 saw him get inducted into the South Carolina Athletic Hall of Fame. The following year, he was inducted into the Cathedral Florida Sports Hall of Fame. In 1983, he was inducted into the Florida Sports Hall of Fame. Three years later, in 1987, he was presented with the Gale Sayers Lifetime Spirit Achievement Award. That same year, the NFL Alumni Organization bestowed upon him "The Order of the Leather Helmet", which is the highest honor they reserve for footballers. Following this, Jones was honored with other honors, such as the "Legend of the Year Award" from the Junior Seay Foundation in 2005.

DEATH

During his later years, Jones battled lung cancer and heart illness. He eventually passed away on June 3rd, 2013, at the age of 74. Jones's reputation as one of the game's most consequential players, however, has only grown since his death. The NFL has a yearly award named after Deacon Jones for the player who had the most sacks that season. Jones had a unique career that will always ensure his place in football folklore.

CHAPTER SEVEN: EMMITT SMITH

Emmitt James Smith III, better known as Emmitt Smith, was born on May 15, 1969, in Pensacola, Florida, United States. He played for the National Football League (NFL) and set a record for most rushing yards in a season in 2002.

A Salvation Army-sponsored football team gave him his first taste of competitive sports when he was only eight years old. He went to Escambia High School, Pensacola, where he participated in both football and track for the Escambia Gators. When Smith was a senior in high school, Escambia won two consecutive state football titles, and Smith had run for 8,804 yards and 106 touchdowns, the latter of which was the second-most in American high school football history at the time. Emmitt started all 49 games he played in for Escambia and finished with a 7.8 ypc average and 45 games with over 100 yards rushing.

He ran for over 2,000 yards in a season twice. Smith was a track and field member of the 4 100 m (42.16 s) relay team.

Smith was honored as the best high school athlete in the country by USA Today and Parade magazine in 1986. In 2007, two decades after Smith had finished high school, the Florida High School Athletic Association (FHSAA) honored him as the "Player of the Century" in Florida high school football. Notably, some college recruiting gurus had claimed that he was too little and too slow to make it as a starting football player at the University of Florida. Smith would go on to prove them all wrong.

COLLEGE CAREER

1987 season

Smith attended the University of Florida on scholarship to play football for coach Galen Hall's Gators for three years (1987–1989). Although he did not start his first two games as a freshman in college in the fall of 1987, he became extra athletic in his week two blowout of Tulsa by rushing for 109 yards on only ten carries, including a 66-yard touchdown run. As a result of his impressive performance that week, he was given the nod to start in the Gators' SEC opener against Alabama at Legion Field.

Smith, making his first collegiate start, carried the ball 39 times for 224 yards and two scores, breaking Florida's all-time single-game running record held by Red Bethea for 57 years. In the seventh game of his freshman year, Smith became the quickest running back in collegiate history to rush for 1,000 yards. His final yardage total was 1,341.He was voted SEC and "National Freshman of the Year", and finished ninth in Heisman Trophy voting.

The year 1988 brought in its wake new challenges for the Gators. Smith sustained an injury and the Gators went on to lose not only the game he was hurt but also the next three games. Starting quarterback Kyle Morris was also hurt, so the team had to go 14 quarters without scoring. The team turned things around after Smith's return and finished the season with a

7-5 record. One of those victories was the 1988 All-American Bowl, which Smith won by scoring on the first play from scrimmage and earning the honor of being recognized as the "most valuable player". Smith's rushing total of 988 yards (not including the bowl game) was the lowest of his college career, and his 110 yards per game average was also his lowest.

In addition, Smith was a participant in the 1989 season. Since then, he has been inducted into the College Football Hall of Fame (2006), the Gator Football Ring of Honor (2004), and the University of Florida Athletic Hall of Fame (1999) as a "Gator Great". He ranked third on the Gainesville Sun's list of the top 100 players in the first 100 years of the Gators' football program in 2006, which was compiled in honor of the program's centennial.

PROFESSIONAL CAREER

He won the Super Bowl for the first time in 1992 while playing for the Dallas Cowboys. Next year, he led his squad to another Super Bowl victory. He established himself with the Dallas Cowboys in his first five seasons as a pro football player, and in 1995, he set a record by playing in the most games with 25 rushing touchdowns. It was his best season, statistically speaking, with 1773 yards rushing and 62 receptions.

As a result of his efforts, his club won the Super Bowl for the third time that year (1995). Success followed him every year, and he was eventually chosen to play in eight Pro Bowls. On October 27th, 2002, his consistency and productivity allowed him to break Walter Payton's all-time record for career running yards. By the time his career ended, he had set NFL records for rushing yards (18,355), touchdowns (164), and attempts (4,409). Despite knowing that he would be let go by the Dallas Cowboys at the end of the 2002 season, he opted to be released, and the team is now paying him $4.9 million. The Arizona Cardinals signed him soon after.

He announced his retirement from the NFL in 2015 shortly before Super Bowl XXXIX kicked off. The same year, he became a studio commentator for the NFL program NFL

Total Access. He expanded his career into property development in 2005. Together with fellow football star Roger Staubach, he formed the investment firm Smith/Cypress Partners LP. In addition, he helped establish ESmith Legacy, a firm that specializes in commercial real estate development and investment management. Not long after he retired, he began making guest appearances on various television programs. He was a judge during the Miss Universe pageant in 2006. He also participated in the popular reality show "Dancing with the Stars", winning the contest with partner Cheryl Burke.

Along with Mike Ditka, Chris Mortensen, and Tom Jackson, he joined ESPN in 2007 as a studio expert for NFL pre-game reporting. The following year, he made a guest appearance on the smash hit US sitcom "How I Met Your Mother". In 2010, he attended Super Bowl XLIV and was invited to flip the coin to determine who would kick off the game between the New Orleans Saints and the Indianapolis Colts. In 2011, he advanced to the second round of the National Heads-Up Poker Championship after beating David Williams. He, however, could not progress further, being defeated by Andrew Robl. He later appeared in the fifteenth season of "Dancing with the Stars, All-Stars," again with Cheryl Burke. He was, however, eliminated from the competition during the early stages.

ACHIEVEMENT & AWARDS

- Career highlights and awards
- 3× Super Bowl champion (XXVII, XXVIII, XXX)
- Super Bowl MVP (XXVIII)
- NFL Most Valuable Player (1993)
- NFL Offensive Rookie of the Year (1990)
- 4× First-team All-Pro (1992–1995)
- 2× Second-team All-Pro (1991, 1996)
- 8× Pro Bowl (1990–1995, 1998, 1999)

- 4× NFL rushing yards leader (1991–1993, 1995)
- 3× NFL rushing touchdowns leader (1992, 1994-1995)
- NFL scoring leader (1995)
- NFL 1990s All-Decade Team
- NFL 100th Anniversary All-Time Team
- PFWA All-Rookie Team (1990)
- Dallas Cowboys Ring of Honor
- Bert Bell Award (1993)
- SEC Most Valuable Player (1989)
- Unanimous All-American (1989)
- 3× First-team All-SEC (1987–1989)
- Florida Football Ring of Honor
- NFL records
- 18,355 rushing yards, a career
- 164 rushing touchdowns, a career
- 4,409 rushing attempts, a career

LEGACY

Smith joined the Phi Beta Sigma fraternity after he was initiated at the University of Florida. During the NFL offseason, he went back to school to finish his degree, and in May of 1996, he received a bachelor's degree in public recreation. Smith is a devout Christian. Smith had a daughter with ex-girlfriend Hope Wilson named Rheagan on November 2nd, 1998. Smith later married Patricia Southall, a former Miss Virginia USA. Their wedding took place on April 22nd, 2000. Together, they have three children: Elijah Alexander James Smith, Skylar Smith, and Emmitt James Smith IV. Smith is the adoptive father of Jasmine

Page Lawrence, Southall's daughter with ex-husband and actor/comedian Martin Lawrence.

Emory, his sibling, had time with the Cowboys and the Packers' practice squads. E. J. Smith, the oldest of Smith's sons, has committed to play football for Stanford University beginning in 2020. This well-known American football player and TV personality, formerly of the Dallas Cowboys, has reportedly agreed to a two-year, $8 million contract with the Arizona Cardinals.

CHAPTER EIGHT: FRANCO HARRIS

Franco Harris, born in the United States on March 7th, 1950, is a former fullback with the Pittsburgh Steelers and the Seattle Seahawks of the National Football League (NFL). After starring for the Penn State Nittany Lions in college football, he was selected thirteenth overall in the 1972 NFL Draft. His first twelve years in the NFL were spent with the Steelers, and his final season was spent with the Seahawks. The Pro Football Hall of Fame inducted him in 1990.

EARLY LIFE

Harris was born in Fort Dix, New Jersey. His father, Cad Harris Sr., fought during World War II and was stationed in Italy. His Italian-born mother, Gina Parenti Harris, joined her American soldier husband in the United States when the war ended. After completing high school in Mount Holly Township, New Jersey, at Rancocas Valley Regional High, Harris earned a degree in Agricultural Economics from Penn State. Harris was primarily a blocker for Penn State's All-American running back, Lydell Mitchell. However, he still rushed for over 2,000 yards and scored 24 times for the Nittany Lions while averaging over 5 yards per carry. He also caught 28 passes for 352 yards and a touchdown. At 197, he was the team's leading scorer.

PROFESSIONAL CAREER

The Sporting News and United Press International named him their league's "Rookie of the Year". He averaged 5.6 yards per run on his 188 carries that year, for 1,055 yards. Additionally, he scored 10 rushing touchdowns and 4 receiving touchdowns. His fans including, most notably "Brigadier General" Frank Sinatra, and the city of Pittsburgh's sizable Italian-American community, nicknamed themselves "Franco's Italian Army" and donned army helmets bearing his number.

Harris was selected for the Pro Bowl nine times in a row (1972–1980) and was named to the All-Pro team in 1977. Harris set a new record by rushing for over a thousand yards in eight consecutive seasons, previously held by Jim Brown. The team won four Super Bowls after the seasons of 1974, 1975, 1978, and 1979, thanks to the strong defense and running back duo of Harris and Rocky Bleier. After gaining 158 yards on the ground and scoring a touchdown on 34 attempts in a 16-6 victory over the Minnesota Vikings on January 12th, 1975, he was named the game's Most Valuable Player and the Super Bowl MVP. Harris made history by becoming the first person of African-American and Italian-American descent to win Super Bowl MVP. For the Steelers, Harris was an integral part of their first four Super Bowl victories. His record of 101 carries for 354 yards and four rushing scores in the Super Bowl remains unbroken. In addition, Harris scored a touchdown in each of the

Steelers' four Super Bowl victories in the 1970s, making him the first player in Super Bowl history to accomplish this feat. Harris maintains that he helped the club achieve its goals (including four Super Bowl triumphs) over a more extended period because he avoided unnecessary contact.

Harris surpassed O. J. Simpson as the all-time leading rusher after Simpson retired at the end of the 1979 season. Harris petitioned the Rooney family for a raise after the 1983 season when he and Walter Payton had both come close to breaking Jim Brown's NFL rushing record. The Rooneys refused to entertain that request as they thought Harris was reaching the end of his career. In 1984, Harris was cut by the Steelers during training camp, and he later signed with the Seattle Seahawks to play for them that year. When he retired after eight games, he had gained 170 yards for the team, 192 yards short of Jim Brown's record.

Harris averaged 4.1 yards per carry throughout his 13-year professional career, leading to a 12,120-yard rushing total (third all-time at the time)on 2,949 carries and 91 rushing touchdowns (then also 3rd). He hauled 307 receptions for 2,287 yards (7.4 yards per catch) and nine touchdowns as a wide receiver. Harris is tied for 10th all-time with Jerome Bettis for most running touchdowns in a career with 91, and his 12,120 rushing yards place him 12th.

Harris was honored by the American Academy of Achievement with the Golden Plate Award in 1984. He was also voted #83 on the list of the 100 Greatest Football Players prepared by The Sporting News in 1999. A life-size statue of Harris was unveiled in the terminal of Pittsburgh International Airport in 2006, courtesy of the Heinz History Center, which houses the Western Pennsylvania Sports Museum. Harris's "Immaculate Reception" is shown in the monument. In 2011, he was placed in the New Jersey Hall of Fame.

POST-FOOTBALL

Harris and Lydell Mitchell were both accomplished athletes at Penn State and are now the proud owners of Super Bakery, a company that has been in business since 1990 and makes healthy school lunches. As of 2006, the company is known as RSuper Foods. The Super

Donut, caused by RSuper foods, is served in many eastern US public schools. In 1996, Harris and Mitchell made headlines by working together to save the Parks Sausage Company, the first African-American-owned company in the United States to go public.

Harris is a paid consultant on the Harrah's/Forest City Enterprises casino proposal in downtown Pittsburgh. Others call him "Franco Harrahs" because of this connection to mock him. Harris was a member of the Pennsylvania delegation that went to the Democratic National Convention in Denver, Colorado, in August of 2008. The convention was held in that city. On December 15th, 2008, Harris cast his ballot for Barack Obama as a Democratic presidential elector for Pennsylvania.

Harris worked at The Meadows Racetrack and Casino in 2011 for a short period before the partnership was terminated in response to Harris' defense of Joe Paterno, his college football coach at Penn State, during the university's child sexual abuse crisis. Harris joined the Pittsburgh Passion as a co-owner in 2011. In the novel "Playing For Pizza" by John Grisham, published in 2008, the fullback for the Parma Panthers, Franco Harris, is given the nickname Franco as a way to pay homage to his hero, who is considered to be the "greatest Italian football player". This is evidence that Franco comes from a mixed ancestry, which may be seen in his appearance.

PERSONAL LIFE

Pete Harris, Harris's brother, and a college football All-American, passed away at 49 from a heart attack on August 15th, 2006. Harris's son Franco "Dok" Harris, declared his run for mayor of Pittsburgh on July 27th, 2009. On November 3rd of that year, he received 25% of the vote in the general election and finished in second place. Franco has been on Penn State's Center for Food Innovation advisory board since 2008. In the fall of 2009, he was appointed a Conti Professor at the School of Hospitality Management. Harris is a part of and financial backer of Penn Staters for Responsible Stewardship, an organization working to remove members of Penn State's board of trustees. Harris was featured in the first episode of Season 3 of “This Is Us”.

CHAPTER NINE: JERRY RICE

EARLY LIFE

Jerry Lee Rice was the sixth of eight children born on October 13th, 1962, in Starkville, Mississippi. He spent his childhood in the nearby town of Crawford, a small and thinly-populated town. Rice's father was a brick mason who constructed houses and worked multiple jobs to support his family. According to Rice, Joe was "a difficult man" who enforced a tight routine on Rice and his siblings. Rice was primarily raised by his mother, Eddie B. Rice and his brothers helped their father build several houses by catching bricks from the tops of scaffolding. The work he did for his father helped him gain an appreciation for the value of hard labor though he decided not to follow in his father's footsteps. The Rice family had financial difficulties, and Rice often went without a "hearty supper on the table" or enough clothes to wear. He and his brothers harvested corn, cotton, and hay to support their families. According to Rice, he was an introverted and unpopular kid.

Rice attended high school at the B. L. Moor Institution in Oktoc, Mississippi. Rice did not participate in any sports during the first two years of high school, despite engaging in regular games of make-believe basketball and football. He was a football fanatic, and spent his time watching games on TV or playing on the sandlot. His mother had deemed football "too tough" for him, so he was not allowed to try out for the squad as a freshman. When the assistant principal spotted Rice and a companion skipping class as sophomores, Rice panicked and ran away. The principal was so taken with Rice's quickness that he reported him to football coach Charles Davis, who promptly invited Rice to join the squad. Rice's mother initially opposed this but eventually gave up because "the more I battled it, the more adamant he was". Rice proved himself to be a versatile athlete who specialized as a forward in basketball and competed in the high jump for track and field. He excelled both on offense and defense. However, it was as a wide receiver that his talents truly shined. Since he didn't have a ride, Rice used to run many miles back to his residence during the offseason before his junior year to enhance his training. Rice primarily played wide receiver and defensive back and had a spectacular junior season.

During his senior year, Rice was chosen as an All-State wide receiver in Mississippi. Moor is such a tiny place that not many statistics on him exist. Sporting journalist Glenn Dickey, however, claims that Rice helped lead his team to a 17-2 record during his senior year after hauling 50 receptions and 30 touchdowns. He and the primary quarterback for Moor, Willie Gillespie, earned the nicknames "Johnny Unitas" and "Raymond Berry" because of their reliability on the field.

At first, Rice had hoped to enroll at Mississippi State University, but the school turned down his application. Over forty NCAA Division I-A institutions reached out to him, including Mississippi State, but none offered him financial aid. His interest in playing for Mississippi Valley State was piqued by the school's passing offense and its head coach, Archie Cooley, who was known as "The Gunslinger". Rice decided to play at Mississippi Valley State after Cooley saw him perform live while visiting the school campus.

COLLEGE CAREER

Rice logged years at Mississippi Valley State University between 1981 and 1984. Before the start of the season, Rice enrolled in summer classes and participated in the new student orientation program at Mississippi Valley State. Present with him there were two of his former B.L. Moor teammates though they both left before training began. As Rice puts it, "I soaked in everything I could" from Gloster Richardson's teachings on receiving.

Rice had a productive rookie year in 1981, finishing with 30 receptions for 428 yards and two scores after entering the league for the first time. Willie Totten, a first-year player at quarterback for Rice, started the 1982 season. A friendship blossomed as they continued to rehearse into the night. According to Cooley, Mississippi Valley State's offense was "unique" since it featured four wideouts lined up on one side of the field. Rice had 66 receptions for 1,133 yards and seven touchdowns during his sophomore season with the team. When Totten teamed up with Rice, they were dubbed "The Satellite Express". The food he was given at Mississippi Valley, however, "was not enough for a grown man". Thus, even though he was successful on the field, he was often forced to rely on friends for sustenance.

In 1983, Rice had a season where many records were smashed. He set several new records including new national bests in receptions (102) and receiving yards (1,980). (1,450). He made first-team All-America in Division I-AA. Against Southern University, he had a then-NCAA record of 24 receptions in a single game. He was dubbed "World" due to his incredible catch rate.

Due to an experiment that took place in August, Cooley now has Totten call all of the plays at the line of scrimmage without using a huddle. This has resulted in even more impressive statistics for the offense. Rice finished his game against Southern with 17 receptions for 199 yards and a touchdown, 17 catches for 294 yards and five touchdowns against Kentucky State, and 15 catches for 285 yards and a touchdown against Jackson State. During the first quarter of the game against Kentucky State, Rice had twelve receptions for touchdowns and scored three touchdowns. In 1984, as a senior, he established new records for receiving yards in Division I-AA (1,845) and receptions in Division I-AA (112). Additionally, the 27 touchdown passes he caught that year set an NCAA record for any division. The 1984 Delta Devils scored over 60 points in each contest on average. In 1984, Rice finished ninth in the Heisman Trophy voting and was chosen to the Division I-AA All-American team.

He was named the game's most valuable player after his four receptions for 101 yards and a 60-yard score in the Blue-Gray Classic all-star game on Christmas Day. Until 2006, when New Hampshire wide receiver David Ball scored his 51st career receiving touchdown, he held the record for most receiving touchdowns in a career. David Ball concluded his career with 301 receptions, 4,693 yards, and 50 touchdowns, setting the record (though some sources have him at 310 receptions, 4,856 receiving yards, and 51 touchdowns). Before Division III Westminster's Scott Pingel recorded his 302nd career reception in 1999, Jerry Rice held the NCAA record for most catches in a career across all divisions. He finished his undergraduate career, having set 18 new national records. Rice pledged allegiance to the Delta Phi chapter of the Phi Beta Sigma fraternity. The football stadium at the university was renamed Rice-Totten Stadium from its previous name, Magnolia Stadium, in 1999.

At that time, Rice was attending an MVS basketball game and ran into a high school classmate, Jackie Mitchell. Before meeting her mother, Rice decided to approach her, and they began a causal relationship. After meeting Rice in person, her mother changed her mind about him and no longer wanted Mitchell to date Rice but instead a boy from Greenville, Mississippi.

PROFESSIONAL CAREER

As a result of Rice's historic season at Mississippi Valley State, he was drafted by the NFL. His 40-yard sprint time was recorded at anywhere from 4.45 to 4.71 seconds, depending on where you looked. He attracted interest from the Dallas Cowboys and the San Francisco 49ers. Before the draft, San Francisco had already won two of the previous four Super Bowls. Later, in Go Long!, Rice revealed that he often "played head games" with himself, doubted his chances of making it to the NFL, and considered switching gears to electronics repair if necessary. Rice told Fox News Digital in 2022, "To be honest, I never thought I was going to get drafted; I downplayed everything because I didn't want that disappointment of getting up here and coming down in disappointment if it didn't happen".

It was the 49ers that picked Rice with the 16th overall pick in the 1985 NFL draft. That year, Rice got off to a slow start but sped up considerably as the season progressed. Rice's second season with the 49ers was the first time he played with Hall of Fame quarterback Joe Montana. During the season, Rice had 86 receptions for 1,570 yards and 15 touchdowns. In 1987, Rice had an even greater season, leading to his being named the league's "Player of the Year" and scoring 23 touchdowns.

After leading the 49ers to the Super Bowl during the 1988–89 season, Rice was voted the NFL's Most Valuable Player for his efforts (MVP). He won two more Super Bowls with the 49ers. Rice played for the San Francisco 49ers, the Oakland Raiders, the Seattle Seahawks, and the Denver Broncos. While playing for the Raiders, Rice reached his fourth Super Bowl, but his team ultimately lost to the Buccaneers.

AWARDS & ACHIEVEMENTS

In 1986, Rice started what would go on to be one of the best stretches for a wide receiver in NFL history. He led the league in receiving yards that season with 1,570 after catching 86 passes. With 15 touchdown catches, he was also the league leader. Rice had a total of

11 consecutive 1,000-yard seasons and 10 or more receiving touchdowns in nine of the next ten years after this one.

One year later, Rice had the most touchdown receptions in a season in NFL history with 22. In 1990, he led the NFL with 100 receptions, the first of four seasons in which he caught at least 100 passes. This was the first of Rice's two championship trophies in this category. He had the most receiving yards in the NFL in 1995 with a record-breaking 1,848. Rice topped the NFL in touchdown receptions as many as six times.

Rice holds the record as the longest-tenured wide receiver in NFL history, with 20 seasons of service. While playing for Oakland and Seattle, he amassed astonishing career totals that made him the most productive wide receiver in NFL history before he retired. Rice has been recognized with many accolades for his exceptional contribution to the sport of football.

PERSONAL LIFE

Rice tied the knot with Jacqueline Bernice Mitchell on September 8th, 1987. The marriage lasted two decades. The couple initiated divorce in June 2007. The divorce was finalized in late December 2009. The couple had three children: Jaqui Bonet (1987), Jerry Rice Jr. (1991), and Jada Symone (1994). In 2009, Jerry Jr. graduated from Menlo School in Atherton, California. Jerry Jr. was a walk-on and a redshirt in his first year at UCLA. Jerry Rice Jr. graduated from UCLA after three seasons with limited playing experience, transferred to UNLV, and was instantly eligible to play. In college, Jerry Jr. started as a wide receiver for the Rebels. Before the 2014 NFL Draft, he participated in a local pro day for the 49ers but was ultimately passed over for selection. Brenden Rice, Jerry's second son, spent two years as a football player at the University of Colorado. According to a press release dated January 1st, 2022, Brenden has decided to enroll at the University of Southern California. On October 21st, 2019, Rice got married to his longtime girlfriend, Latisha Pelayo.

AFTER FOOTBALL

Rice appeared on the popular dance reality show"Dancing with the Stars" during the 2005–2006 season. Partnering with dancer Anna Trebunskaya, he made it to the final round but ultimately lost to singer Drew Lachey and his partner Cheryl Burke. Rice played the character of Hal Gore in the 2009 film "Without a Paddle: Nature's Calling". That same year, he made a cameo appearance on the sitcom "Rules of Engagement" as himself in the episode "Lyin' King." Rice has authored two biographies. "Rice" (co-authored with Michael Silver) was published in 1996 while "Go Long: My Journey Beyond the Game and the Fame" (co-authored with Brian Curtis) was published in 2007. In 2019, Rice co-authored a book with Randy O. Williams titled "America's Game: The NFL at 100" to mark the 100th year of the National Football League. A video game for the Wii titled "Jerry Rice & Nitus' Dog Football was published on August 16th, 2011, and featured both Rice and Nitus. During the 2014 and 2016 Pro Bowls, Rice captained the "Team Rice" alumni squad. To promote the importance of giving blood, Rice University joined forces with the American Red Cross in 2022.

Rice has been a golfer for nearly 20 years and used to get up early during his football career to play golf. On April 15 and 16, 2010, he used a sponsor's exemption to play in the Nationwide Tour's Fresh Express Classic at TPC Stonebrae. Rice was one of the 152 golfers who started the tournament, but he was the last to finish. He was 17 shots over par and finished in 151st place. He captained the victorious team from Puerto Rico on The Big Break.

CHAPTER TEN: JOE MONTANA

It is understandable why Tom Brady would get the most attention in discussions regarding the greatest quarterbacks of all time. However, before Brady attained stardom, it was Joe Montana that reigned supreme as the greatest quarterback. Montana was a popular figure in the National Football League (NFL) for many years. He even has the Super Bowl rings to prove it. Let's reflect on the years spent in the NFL by the quarterback who led the 49ers to become the most successful team of the 1980s.

EARLY LIFE

He was born in New Eagle, Pennsylvania, a borough of Washington County in the state's western corner, to Joseph Clifford Montana Sr. (1932-2017) and Theresa Marie Bavuso Montana (1935-2004). In his youth, he resided in Monongahela, a coal-mining community located about 40 kilometers (25 miles) south of Pittsburgh. Montana showed interest in athletics very early on. It was his father that introduced him to football. At the age of eight, with encouragement from his dad, Montana began playing youth football. Legend has it that Montana Sr. falsified his son's age to get him into the league. While Montana excelled in baseball and football, his favorite sport during those formative years was basketball. His father, Montana Sr., had formed a basketball team in the area, and his son played for the squad. They competed in local tournaments and used the armory for practice.

Montana attended Waverly Elementary, Finleyville Junior High (now called Finleyville Middle School), and Ringgold High School for his elementary and senior schooling respectively. Montana participated in three sports at Ringgold: football, baseball, and basketball. At the 1973 WPIAL Class AAA boys' basketball championship, Ringgold won and Montana was chosen an all-state player for his outstanding effort. The North Carolina State University extended a scholarship offer to Montana based on his play as a senior, and while he ultimately decided against attending NC State, Montana gave the Wolfpack's football and basketball programs substantial consideration.

Montana was a backup for the high school football squad for his first two years. Montana was the starting quarterback for the Ringgold Rams, a position he had held since he was a junior. After two years in the post, Montana graduated from high school as a Parade magazine's All-American team member. Montana's junior year performance versus Monessen High School stands out as one of his best from high school. Despite Monessen's late touchdown, which tied the game, Montana's performance caught the eye of college scouts. This was especially true at Notre Dame. Montana had three passing touchdowns and one rushing touchdown on 223 yards and 12 completions in 22 attempts. After being awarded a scholarship, Montana decided to attend Notre Dame. Montana's childhood hero Terry Hanratty played a pivotal role in his decision to enroll at Notre Dame. Ringgold High School's football stadium was dubbed "Joe Montana Stadium" in 2006, 32 years after Montana had graduated.

COLLEGE CAREER

In the fall of 1974, when Montana first enrolled at Notre Dame, Ara Parseghian led the Fighting Irish football team. Two of Notre Dame's three NCAA titles (1966 and 1973) came under Parseghian's watch. Parseghian's success as a coach allowed him to attract many excellent athletes. Although he was a highly touted recruit, Montana only played in a handful of games for the Notre Dame freshman squad in 1974 due to the school's policy of prohibiting freshmen from participating in varsity practices or games. It was during his second year that he made substantial contributions to the Notre Dame football squad.

The resignation of Parseghian on December 15th, 1974, owing to health issues led to the appointment of Dan Devine as the new coach Montana had a good spring practice in 1975 despite his lack of playing time the year before. Devine told his wife, "I'm going to start Joe Montana in the final spring game" after seeing Montana perform so well. Devine apparently told her, "He's the one who's going to feed our family for the next five years" when she asked, "Who's Joe Montana?" Devine proved to be right. In 1978, when Montana was a fifth-year senior, he led Notre Dame to a miraculous victory over the Pitt Panthers and nearly pulled off a similar upset against USC, the Fighting Irish's main rival. After falling behind 24-6 in the second half, Montana led a fourth-quarter comeback that put Notre Dame ahead by 25-24 with 45 seconds remaining. However, the Trojans returned and won on a last-second field goal.

Notre Dame again played Houston in the Cotton Bowl on January 1st, 1979. In retrospect, Joe Montana's performance in the infamous "Chicken Soup Game" stands as one of the highlights of his brilliant football career. Montana's body temperature dropped to 96 degrees Fahrenheit (35.6 degrees Celsius) in the cold and wind during the second quarter, forcing him to battle hypothermia. With Houston leading 20-12 at halftime, Notre Dame's medical staff kept Montana in the locker room to administer chicken soup, warm intravenous fluids, and blankets. Montana came back onto the field at the end of the third quarter, with Houston up 34-12. Notre Dame came from behind to win 35-34 thanks to the three touchdowns scored by Montana and the Irish in the game's final eight minutes.

PROFESSIONAL CAREER

He had a fruitful collegiate experience and ultimately earned his degree from Notre Dame. Soon after completing his degree, Montana was drafted by the San Francisco 49ers of the NFL and played in all 16 games for the team that season. By 1981, Montana and coach Bill Was had established themselves as a formidable duo. Under their direction, the San Francisco 49ers defeated the Dallas Cowboys in the National Football Conference championship game. It was one of the most memorable NFL performances in the fourth quarter.

The following year, in Super Bowl XVI, the club met the Cincinnati Bengals, and the talented quarterback guided his team to victory with an outstanding performance. When Montana won the Super Bowl, he joined Peyton Manning as one of only two quarterbacks in history to accomplish both feats. In 1984, Montana returned to the Pro Bowl after leading his team to victories over the New York Giants and Chicago Bears. In Super Bowl XIX, his squad played against the Dolphins and set a record of the highest passing yards in a game with 558. Never before had a team won 15 games in a season until Montana helped his team accomplish this extraordinary feat.

1985-1989

Montana sustained a serious injury to his lumbar spinal disc that resulted in an emergency surgery. He, however, bounced back quickly and shone in the game against the St. Louis Cardinals. That season, he played only eight games but still managed to register a career-high interception of 14. In 1987, Montana reached a career-high point by passing for 3054 yards without an interception, setting an NFL record that still stands today. Super Bowl XXIII was a second chance for the squad, and they made the most of it by beating the

Minnesota Vikings and the Chicago Bears. The following year, under his leadership, his team had a phenomenal season, culminating in Super Bowl XXIV, where he became the first player to win the game MVP award three times.

1990-1995

In 1990, the 49ers remained undefeated at home under Montana's direction. That year, Sports Illustrated duly recognized him as their "Athlete of the Year". Due to an elbow injury, however, he could not contribute much to the 49ers' offense in 1991–1992. In 1994, after overcoming his injuries, Montana made a comeback. He participated in two games, including a legendary matchup with John Elway on Monday Night Football and against his old team, the 49ers, and Steve Young.

RETIREMENT

Montana announced his retirement on April 18th, 1995, in Justin Herman Plaza in San Francisco, in front of a massive crowd. John Madden, Eddie DeBartolo, Jr., and others spoke at the occasion, which was televised live on local television. The program also featured recollections from Montana's time with the 49ers and comments from some of his old teammates. MC duties for the night were handled by none other than Bill Walsh. Former 49ers backup quarterback Steve Bono took over for Montana with the Chiefs.

PERSONAL LIFE

Montana has been married thrice. During his second semester at Notre Dame in 1974, he married his high school girlfriend, Kim Moses; they separated after three years of marriage. He wed Cass Castillo in 1981, before divorcing her in 1984. He met his future wife, Jennifer Wallace, on the set of a commercial for Schick razors. They tied the knot in 1985. They had four children: Alexandra (born October 10th, 1985), Elizabeth (born December 20th, 1986), Nate (born October 3rd, 1989), and Nicholas (born October 10th, 1995). His boys also played football for De La Salle High School. Both Nate (from Notre Dame) and Nick (from Tulane) moved schools and ended up as undrafted free agents playing for West Virginia Wesleyan (having transferred from the University of Washington and Mt. San Antonio College). After his ex-wife Moses "sold a bundle of letters and mementoes from [Montana's] college days at Notre Dame," he filed suit against Moses and a Dallas auction company in 2008 for "violating his 'copyright and privacy rights.'"

Montana resides in San Francisco. In 2009, he listed his 500-acre (2.0 km2) home in Calistoga, California, for $49 million; by January 2012, the price had been dropped to $35 million. Apart from making wine under the label Montagia, he also has a stable full of horses. Montana is a big supporter of the Make-A-Wish Foundation and other humanitarian organizations.

LEGACY

Montana's name has been brought up frequently when discussing the NFL's all-time greats. He was the starting quarterback on the NFL's 1980s All-Decade Team, but his greatness extended beyond that decade. Montana was also a member of both the 75th and 100th Anniversary Teams. The 49ers also announced that they would retire his jersey number, 16.

Montana became known as "Joe Cool" for maintaining composure under pressure. Legend has it that before he led the Niners on their game-winning 92-yard drive against the Bengals in Super Bowl XLVI, he showed John Candy to his teammates in the stands. Two MVP awards and three Super Bowl MVP awards came his way, thanks to his comeback victories. There were six times in his career that Montana was named to the All-Pro team, and his productivity was above average for his period. Montana had the highest completion percentage in the league five times in his career. Harmonized efficiency and serenity – that's how you earn a place in history. Montana is one player that the sport of football shall remain forever indebted to.

CHAPTER ELEVEN: STEVE YOUNG

Steve Young's football career is one filled with so many accomplishments. He's known to be among the highest-rated quarterbacks in the history of American football. He played in the NFL for about 15 seasons in the San Francisco 49ers, bay buccaneers, and USFL Express, to mention just a few. Like every other NFL star, Steve won about three super bowl awards and MVP awards and was included in the hall of Fame. How did he start his career? We're going to find out.

EARLY LIFE & CHILDHOOD

Steve Young was born on October 11, 1961, in Salt lake city, Utah, USA. He was the oldest among the five children of Legrande Young, an attorney, and Sherry Steed. While growing up, their family moved to Greenwich, Connecticut, in 1969. However, Steve wasn't so happy about it. He had once, in an interview, spoken about his separation anxiety syndrome. As a boy, Steve already loved sports, especially football, basketball, and baseball. He engaged in various sports activities in which he excelled. Steve Young was the great-great-great-grandson of Brigham Young, the founder of the Mormon church. Steven and his siblings were raised in Christian ways, adhering strictly to the rules of faith.

HIGH SCHOOL

When he reached high school age, he enrolled in Greenwich high school in Connecticut. As a lover of football, Steve joined the school football team cardinals. During his junior year, he started his career as a quarterback in the team, And to everyone's amazement, he performed excellently well. He was awarded the ALL-FCIAC west division first-team honors. In his senior year, Steve had gotten 13 touchdowns, had about 41 percent throws from 1220 yards, and ran the ball 267 times for nearly 1,928 yards. He was the team's captain, and at this point, he was the best quarterback they've got. With many victories, his team wanted him to join them in the celebration by partying and drinking alcohol, but Steve will not join them because of his Christian background. In 1979, he graduated.

COLLEGE FOOTBALL CAREER

In 1980, Steve Young got admitted into Brigham Young university, even after receiving several scholarships from other universities that wanted Steve to come to play for their team. He tried to follow in his father's footsteps as he had once played for the BYU team. When Steven joined the team, their game pattern took time to adapt. The coach had requested 50 passes be made per game play. Steve couldn't meet up, so he was on the team's eight-string quarterback. Fortunately, one day, his performance in training impressed the coach, and that's how he could play in other matches. During the second season, Steve was second to Jim MacMahon. Unfortunately, Jim was injured in a game which led Steve to step in—leading the team to win various matches. They were selected to play against Ohio State in the 1982 holiday bowl game. Although, they lost the match. Steve came in second in the 1983 Heisman trophy vote. He graduated in 1983 with the record as the only player with the highest single-season passes, a percentage of about 71.3%. A remarkable score, you would say.

PROFESSIONAL CAREER

Starting his career in the NFL league, the Cincinnati Bengals already had plans of drafting Steve in their team. The USFL Los Angeles express also planned to draft him with a mouth-watering contract of $40 million. It was the most significant contract in NFL history back then. Steve chose the (USFL) team. He played well for the team, leading them to several victories, but Steve left due to the management's financial crises.

He got into the Tampa bay buccaneers team in 1985 with a $6 million contract. The team could have performed better due to its structure and players, so Steve couldn't commit to expectations. He was sold to the San Francisco 49ers in 1987. Playing as Jon Montana's backup in case Montana sustained any injury. Coach Walsh wanted Steve since he was the young and vibrant quarterback. In the early seasons, Steve's play pattern was different from what the team and fans expected because it differed from their play style. It made him have issues playing well for the team. But later in the seasons, he performed well and stepped in for Montana after sustaining a back injury. Montana left after the second season, leaving Steve as the team's only quarterback. Steve had an excellent performance and won his Fourth consecutive ranking in the NFL's top quarterbacks. After their win against San Diego, a score of 49-26, with Steve making six touchdowns and rushing more yards, he was named the super bowl's MVP of the season.

OFF THE FIELD

Steve Young married Barbara Graham in 2000. They had four lovely children and lived peacefully. Steve retired from football after his marriage. Aside from football, Steve was an attorney. He studied law and graduated from Brigham Young university in 1993, carrying out legal duties for his foundation. Before the birth of his son, Steven decided to retire from football; he was a content writer, as he wrote his autobiography titled " my life behind a spiral." Many say he was inspired to write it due to his son's birth and family.

POST CAREER

After retirement in 1999, Steve went into the business sector. He co-founded Huntsman Gay Global Capital in 2007; he later became the Director. Steve founded an NGO called "Forever Young Foundation" they specialize in charitable activities for society, supporting sports activities at the San Francisco school to help the children and Americans at large. Steve's love for sports led him to become an ambassador for the Salt Lake Olympic committee in the 2002 Olympic winter games.

LEGACIES

Steve Young's exceptional performance as a quarterback player made him the only best in the history of the NFL. He is a player to have won MVP twice, a Super Bowl, and his name was recorded in the hall of Fame. He has completed 2,667 passes from over 30,000 yards and 232 touchdowns. He also had 43 rush touchdowns. He has a passing rate of about 96.8% throughout his career, and he's the second-rated retired player after Tony Romo. By the 2022 estimate, his net worth was about $222 million. Steve's list of accomplishments is endless.

CHAPTER TWELVE: TERRELL OWENS

Terrell Owens was a very talented player. He was nicknamed T.O. as the initials from his name. Well-known for his outstanding skills on the field, he played as a wide receiver in the National football league (NFL) for over 12 seasons. Terrell Owens's performance made his name among the world's best wide receivers in football history. He was also nominated for the Pro Bowls several times. Let's take a look at his life and journey into football.

EARLY LIFE AND CHILDHOOD

Terrell Owens was born in 1973 in Alabama—his father, L.C. Russell, and mother, Marilyn Heard. Unfortunately, Owen's father abandoned his family after he divorced his wife. Owens grew up with his three siblings, all trained by their mother and grandmother. Owens had always had a passion for football; he was very passionate and always admired the legendary NFL player Jerry Rice. Back then, he participated in various sports activities. Owens went to Benjamin Russell high school. Terrell Owens was known for his hot temper; there have been instances where he had heated confrontations with his coaches and players on the field.

A notable instance was in 2004 when he argued with his team San Francisco 49ers. His attitude made sports news media criticize him for not having sportsman behavior. Terrell Owens was from a poor background but rose to become a great individual in his Career.

HIGH SCHOOL

Going to Benjamin Russell high school in 1988, Owens, with his already developed passion for football and basketball, joined the school football team, although he couldn't play then since he wasn't very good. Even with several attempts in his senior season, he failed. His coach had to advise him not to quit football. Owens's determination to become a professional football motivated him. While others were busy partying and resting, Owens was constantly training himself till he became talented. His determination fueled consistently paid off. After improving himself, he participated in other sports, such as basketball and baseball.

COLLEGE FOOTBALL CAREER

After high school, he enrolled in college, attending the University of Tennessee in Chattanooga. Owens joined the college football team called Mocs. By then, he was playing football, basketball, and baseball together. It was fortunate that his sports director didn't object to his options. Owen's football career came into the limelight while he was playing for his team as he set records by catching 38 passes from 724 yards distance, and together with about eight touchdowns in his sophomore year. He also caught 34 passes from a 357-yard distance and three touchdowns. By this time, his skills were already developed, and he was getting into the limelight.

PROFESSIONAL CAREER

His Career in the NFL started in 1996. Owens was drafted into the San Francisco 49ers team. Owens got to see his childhood mentor, Jerry rice. His notable game was when he made a 45-yard touchdown against the Cincinnati Bengals, ending the game in a win. He ensured 13 victories in total for the team. Due to Owen's misconduct, he was penalized. He later left in 2003 and joined the Philadelphia eagles.

He played excellently well for the team by leading them to several victories, such as against the Ravens, and even took the team to the Super Bowl. But his attitude toward the management led to his suspension. He played for the Dallas Cowboys in 2006 and signed a three year contract. Fortunately, he was able to complete this contract. He played well for the team having over 15 touchdowns and over 1000 wide receiving yards. But his attitude got the better of him. After his contract with the team, he was signed into the buffalo bills, where he earned about 98-yard touchdowns. However, he didn't perform to their expectations, so he left the team. Between 2010 to 2012, he played several games for both Cincinnati Bengals and Allen Wranglers. He caught several touchdowns, but injuries held him down even though he created notable records for himself in those teams.

OFF THE FIELD

Terrell Owens was a father of four children, even though they all were from different mothers. He always had issues with being taken to court by his girlfriend due to a lack of payment for child support. When off the field, Owens was into music; one of the songs he released was titled "I'm back." He was already an ambassador to different brands, and he appeared in various commercials, T.V. shows, and even movies. He played a role in the film "Any given Sunday." The ESPY Awards commercials. He also hosted his T.V. reality show called "The T.O. show," where he invited celebrities and talked about his life and society. Despite so many controversies surrounding him, he still had a notable social media presence.

POST CAREER

Terrell Owens didn't retire from football. He was seen signing different contracts with different teams. At Allen Wranglers, Owens signed a deal as a co-owner of the team, and he played for the team where he caught 3 passes for 53 yards and 3 touchdowns. However, the management took the deal away from him because he couldn't show more effort to improve the team. He went to sign a deal with the Seattle Seahawks in 2012, and in 2015, he said in an interview that he wasn't going to retire from football. He made some moves to come back into the NFL league after his last NFL game in 2010 but ultimately retired for good.

LEGACIES

Terrell Owens was the super talented player the NFL had ever seen. Having up to 6 pro bowls, he got 3 NFL receiving touchdowns leader awards. He had exceptionally accomplished several achievements; he made over 1000 receptions, 15,932 receiving yards, and 153 touchdowns in his history. Even with a series of injuries he sustained, Owens still got back on the field. Although he was known for his violent behaviors and having heated arguments with his management and team players but in all this, Terrell Owens's name will not be forgotten in the history of American football.

CHAPTER THIRTEEN: ODELL BECKHAM JR.

Considered to be one of the most controversial players in the NFL because of how he continuously breaks basic NFL rules, Odell Beckham Jr. has become one of the most popular names in the NFL today.

EARLY LIFE

Odell Cornelius Beckham Jr, known by his initials OBJ, was born November 5, 1992, in Baton Rouge, Louisiana, USA. He came from a very sporty family, as his parents, both the biological pair and his stepfather, were all accomplished athletes. In many of his interviews in his later life, he mentions that he was raised to be an athlete by his parents. Beckham was the first child, with a younger sister, Jasmine, and brother, Kordell.

HIGH SCHOOL

Isidore Newman School in New Orleans, Louisiana, was fortunate to have him as a student because he excelled academically there. As was to be expected, Beckham was a letterman in three different sports: football, basketball, and track. He excelled naturally in all of the sports in which he participated. In addition to this, he followed in his mother's footsteps and took part in jumping competitions. Beckham achieved a personal best jump of 6.83 meters during the long jump competition that took place during the 2010 Newman Invitational. He won the silver medal for his performance.

Beckham was a soccer player and came close to being selected for the junior national squad at one point. David Beckham, an English soccer player, served as an inspiration for him, and one may make the connection between their names given that they are so similar. Despite this, he chose not to follow his goal of playing soccer abroad since he believed that he could be successful in sports in his native country as well.

Beckham was ranked as the nation's sixth-best wide receiver and the 40th-best athlete overall in the year that he graduated from high school. He was eligible for a number of financial aid packages, but he ultimately decided to attend Louisiana State University rather than any of the other schools. In 2011, he also participated in the U.S. Army All-American Bowl.

COLLEGE CAREER

OBJ played for the Louisiana State University's football team, the Tigers, and he was sure to keep his amazing rolling. In 2011, during his freshman year, he started 9 of 14 games he featured in. At the end of that year, he was named in the freshman All-SEC selection.

His sophomore year was no different, as he played 13 out of 14 games that season. Most memorable for him that year, he had an 89-yard punt return touchdown in the fourth quarter to help tie the game late against SEC rivals Ole Miss. He led the Tigers to the Chick-fil-A Bowl qualifications that year.

In OBJ's senior year, he partnered with his teammate, Jarvis Landry, forming the most explosive wide receiver duo in the league. He won the 2013 Paul Hornung Award, which is given to the most versatile player in major league football. OBJ was an excellent wide receiver and returner. After his junior year, he left school and got into the 2014 drafts.

PROFESSIONAL CAREER

OBJ was a member of the football team known as the Tigers at Louisiana State University, and he made it a point to maintain his incredible play throughout his career. In 2011, while he was still a freshman, he started nine out of the 14 games that he participated in. At the conclusion of that academic year, he was selected for inclusion in the freshman All-SEC team.

It was business as usual for him during his sophomore year, as he participated in 13 of the season's 14 games. The moment that stands out the most for him from that season was when he scored a touchdown on a punt return after covering 89 yards late in the game against Ole Miss, an opponent from the same conference. He guided the Tigers to the qualifying for the Chick-fil-A Bowl that particular year.

During OBJ's senior season, he and his fellow colleague Jarvis Landry formed what was widely considered to be the most dynamic wide receiver tandem in the league. He was awarded the Paul Hornung Award in 2013, which is presented to the player in major league football who has the most versatility. OBJ was a fantastic wide receiver as well as a return man. After completing his junior year, he decided not to continue his education and entered the 2014 draft instead.

Controversies

If you know Beckham, you know that there is usually some sort of controversy surrounding whatever he is doing. Despite his talent, the NFL is constantly filing and suspending him for his defiant play. A dance celebration in the Giants' season opener against the Cowboys cost him a $12,154 fine in 2016. A blindside hit on safety Kenny Vaccaro the next week cost him a $36,000 punishment.

Beckham threw a punch at Ravens CB Marlon Humphrey in 2019 after he had joined the Browns, and Humphrey responded by choking Beckham. For their extreme disrespect, both players were fined $14,000. Every time OBJ broke uniform laws, he was hit with a fine.

Beckham's father had an online outburst over how his son was being utilized in Brown's attack, and the team decided they couldn't handle the publicity, so they released him.

OFF THE FIELD

Beckham Jr. views paying the multiple penalties he receives as a public service. He's donated time and money to a wide variety of charities, including those that fund cancer research, fight hunger in the United States, grant wishes for children with terminal illnesses, and more.

Beckham and his wife, Lauren Wood, welcomed their first child in February 2022. In 2018, Beckham, a devout Christian, even got baptized in the river Jordan. He considers his family and friends his closest possessions.

CHAPTER FOURTEEN: JUNIOR SEAU

The late American football linebacker Tiaina Baul "Junior" Seau Jr. (born January 19, 1969) passed away on May 2, 2012. (NFL). Because of his fiery performance, he was recognized by his peers as a 10-time All-Pro, a 12-time Pro Bowler, and a member of the NFL's All-Decade Team in the 1990s. A year after his death, he received posthumous induction into the Pro Football Hall of Fame.

Junior Seau was drafted by the San Diego Chargers in 1990, with the fifth overall pick of that year's draft. Throughout the next 20 years, he was one of the best linebackers in NFL history, thanks to his doggedness, leadership, and overall effectiveness on the field.

Seau is a former USC Trojans football player who grew up in Oceanside, California. The San Diego Chargers picked him up at No. 5 in the 1990 NFL Draft. Seau led the Chargers to Super Bowl XXIX in his first 13 seasons as a starter for the team, was traded to the Miami Dolphins for three years, and finished his career with the New England Patriots. Once he retired, the Chargers honored him by retiring his number 55 and inducting him into the team's Hall of Fame.

At the age of 43, Seau shot himself in the chest and took his own life in 2012. The National Institutes of Health (NIH) later concluded that Seau had chronic traumatic encephalopathy (CTE), a disease that has been discovered in the brains of several deceased ex-NFL players. Repetitive head trauma is blamed for this illness, which has been linked to dementia, aggression, and despair.

EARLY YEARS

On January 19, 1969, Seau was born in Oceanside, California. He is the fifth child of Tiaina Seau Sr. and Luisa Mauga Seau of Aunu'u, American Samoa. The grandfather of Tiaina Sr. was the leader of a Pago Pago community. Luisa worked at the Camp Pendleton commissary and a laundromat, and Tiaina Sr. worked at a rubber factory and as a school custodian in Southern California. The Seaus returned to American Samoa for a while after Seau was born, and he didn't learn to speak English until he was seven. Seau and his three siblings were forced to use the family's one-car garage as a bedroom when their parents could no longer afford a proper dwelling.

Seau earned varsity letters in football, basketball, and track and field while a student at Oceanside High School. In high school, Seau was a two-way starter on the football team, playing both linebacker and tight end. He was the team's offensive MVP his senior year and helped lead the Oceanside Pirates to the San Diego 2A title. Seau was named to the Parade high school all-American team. As a senior, he led his basketball team to the San Diego Section championship and was named the CIF Player of the Year. He was a key member of the squad that took first place at the 1987 Lt. James Mitchell Tournament and third at the 1987 Mt. Carmel Invitational. When in high school, he dominated the competition in the shot put, winning the Avocado League title. Seau's 3.6 GPA landed him on California's all-academic team.

COLLEGE CAREER

Seau went to the University of Southern California after finishing high school (USC). His SAT score of 690 put him 10 points below USC's threshold for freshman eligibility. Therefore, he missed out on his first year of college sports.

Seau told Sports Illustrated: "I was labeled a dumb jock. At USC, I transitioned from a four-sport athlete to a regular student. To my relief, I identified my genuine circle of support. No one defended me — not my family, not my best friend, not even our neighbor. My parents heard it from multiple people at church: "We told you he was never going to make it." Jealousy and a desire to prevent others from succeeding are common attitudes among Samoans." Because of this, he felt obligated to apologize to his coaches, professors, and the principal at Oceanside High.

His final two years at USC were 1988 and 1989, both of which he spent as a letter winner. In 1989, he recorded 19 sacks and was named to the All-America first team.

PROFESSIONAL CAREER

San Diego Chargers

After three years with the Trojans, Seau declared for the 1990 NFL Draft following his junior year and was selected fifth overall by Bobby Beathard's San Diego Chargers. Seau's wild actions on the field earned him the nickname "Tasmanian Devil," and he rapidly rose to stardom with the Chargers. He was the team's most recognizable player and a cultural symbol for the city of San Diego.

After 13 years with the team, Seau's number was retired by the San Diego Chargers. In his first season as a starter, Seau had 85 tackles and was chosen as an alternate to the 1991 Pro Bowl. In 1991, Seau recorded 129 tackles and seven sacks, earning him a spot in the Pro Bowl for the first time in what would become a record-setting 12 straight appearances. In addition, he received honors as the NFL's Defensive MVP from the Newspaper Enterprise Association, AFC Defensive Player of the Year from the Associated Press, NFL Alumni Linebacker of the Year from the NFL, and NFLPA AFC Linebacker of the Year from the NFL Players Association.

Throughout the next 11 years, he never missed more than 13 starts with the Chargers and had his best season with 155 tackles. United Press International honored Seau as NFL Defensive Player of the Year that season, and his team went on to play in Super Bowl XXIX. He played the 1994 AFC Championship Game with a pinched nerve in his neck and still recorded 16 tackles, helping the team to a 17-13 victory over the Pittsburgh Steelers. His last season with the Chargers was in 2002 when he recorded a career-low 83 tackles and missed his final Pro Bowl due to an ankle ailment.

Miami Dolphins

When the Miami Dolphins needed a defensive back, they acquired Seau on April 16, 2003, in exchange for a draft pick. With a Dolphins team that finished 9-7 that year, he was a key defensive contributor, starting 15 games. In 2004, however, Seau was only able to play in eight games and finished with 68 tackles and one sack due to a damaged pectoral muscle. He played in the first seven games for the Dolphins in 2005, starting five of them. On November 24, however, he was placed on injured reserve with a torn Achilles tendon. Seau was cut by the Dolphins on March 6, 2006.

New England Patriots

At a tearful press conference on August 14, 2006, Seau declared his retirement. Although he had no intention of stopping his work, he celebrated the occasion as if it were his graduation. He claimed he was only entering a new chapter in his life.

Just four days after his release from the hospital, Seau signed with the New England Patriots and was back on the field. He started 10 of the Patriots' first 11 games and finished the season with 69 tackles before injuring his right arm against the Chicago Bears. On November 27, he was transferred to the IR with an injury.

Seau re-signed with the Patriots on May 21, 2007, ahead of the upcoming 2007 season. Seau was elected a captain with the Patriots back in September of 2007. His contributions that year were crucial to the Patriots' perfect regular season. During the 2007 season, he played in all 16 games for the Patriots and started four of them. He also started both playoff games leading up to Super Bowl XLII against the New York Giants. The Patriots' perfect season concluded with a loss in the Super Bowl to the Giants.

The Patriots re-signed Seau after a string of late-season injuries in 2008. In two out of the four games he participated in, he was a starter. A fan who tackled Junior Seau as he stood on the New England sideline during their home game against the Arizona Cardinals on December 22, 2008, was arrested for trespassing and assault and battery. Seau claimed he did not feel intimidated and that the fan was just overly enthusiastic about the game.

After taking physicals and working out with the organization, NFL Network reported on October 7, 2009, that Seau and the New England Patriots had reached an "agreement in principle" for a fourth one-year deal. The contract was formally signed on October 13. In 2009, he was a reserve linebacker for the Patriots and played in seven games, contributing 14 tackles.

RETIREMENT

On January 13, 2010, while doing an interview on Inside the NFL, Junior Seau stated that he would be retiring from the National Football League for good.

CHAPTER FIFTEEN: DEANDRE HOPKINS

EARLY LIFE

DeAndre Hopkins was born on June 6, 1992, in Central, South Carolina. His father, Harris Hopkins, was a full-time drug dealer hence, having been placed under intensive care. Unfortunately, the night he left probation, he was involved in a car accident that took his life. At that time, DeAndre was only 5 months old.

So, DeAndre and his siblings were left to be raised by their single mother. She had to work numerous jobs to feed the little ones and ensure they did not feel the absence of their dad. When DeAndre was little, his mum nicknamed him "Nuke." This was because he always chewed his NUK mouth pacifier when given to him. This name stuck to his general life, even till the present day.

HIGH SCHOOL

He attended D.W. Daniel High School and participated in football, basketball, and track events. However, most of his efforts and interests were in football, as he recorded 7 receptions for 1,266 yards and 18 touchdowns on offense and 28 interceptions, returning five for touchdowns on defense. On the basketball team, he played as both a shooting and point guard and recorded 1,453 career points.

During his time playing for his high school's football team, DeAndre helped maintain a 37-4 record. In his senior season in 2009-2010, he won the Lions their third South Carolina State Championship. He had an excellent career in high school and was named the 12th-best wide receiver in the nation and the State of South Carolina.

COLLEGE CAREER

DeAndre Hopkins enrolled at Clemson University in 2010 and joined the football team, the Clemson Tigers. His debut game was against North Texas, where the Tigers won 34-10. DeAndre recorded two receptions for 23 receiving yards in that game. At the end of his freshman year, he was Clemson's leading receiver for Clemson, with 52 receptions for 637 receiving yards and 4 receiving touchdowns. He also continued to play basketball in his first year of college. He was on the Tigers' team.

In 2011, during his Sophomore year, he had a big up to his career, and so did the Tigers. They finished with a 10-4 season record, but he was the second place in the season's receivers ranking. Regardless of how good of a season the Tigers were having, they recorded the worst loss in their history. They lost 70-33 to West Virginia.

By the time DeAndre was in his junior year in 2012, he had totaled 206 receptions for 3000 yards, 27 touchdowns, and scored 18 times. In his junior season, DeAndre set a conference-best of 82 catches in 1,405 yards and 18 touchdowns. This earned him First-team All-Conference honors for the ACC. DeAndre skipped his senior year and went for the NFL drafts.

PROFESSIONAL CAREER

After DeAndre left Clemson, he was invited to the NFL pre-draft combine because of the very high prospects he showed. He completed all his drills excellently but failed the three-cone drill due to an apparent calf injury.

DeAndre was the 27th pick in the first round of the 2013 NFL drafts. He was chosen by the Houston Texans, making him the second wide receiver ever to get drafted in the first round. DeAndre made his NFL debut against the San Diego Chargers, which the Texans won 31-28. DeAndre made 5 receptions for 55 yards in that game. At the end of his rookie season, he was listed in the NFL Rookie team of the season for 2013.

In the 2015 season, DeAndre was ranked 19th in the NFL top 100 by other players in the league. By the next year, DeAndre had already become a popular name in the league, but he had a lot of twists that season. In July of that year, DeAndre missed a lot of his training while waiting for his new contract. Later on, he had a little scuffle with the authorities after wearing Yeezy custom cleats to a game. He was fined $6,000 for the uniform law breach. DeAndre finished off 2016 with 78 receptions for 954 yards and four touchdowns- his worst since his rookie season.

DeAndre was well known for his acrobatic catches, which seemed to be a problem for the defenses he faced. He was quick with the ball and had slick body control.

In 2020, DeAndre Hopkins was traded to the Arizona Cardinals, and the media believed the Texans were being robbed. He made his debut that same year against the San Francisco 49ers, in which he dropped a career-high 14 receptions for 151 yards in the 24–20 win. That year, he was awarded his fifth Pro Bowl and ranked 8th on the players' top 100 list.

His career continued to go steady, but in 2022, DeAndre was accused of using performance-enhancing drugs and was therefore suspended for 6 games. The 7th game saw his return, making 10 receptions for 103 yards. He finished with 64 receptions for 717 receiving yards and three receiving touchdowns. DeAndre is the youngest player to reach 700 catches, a record that was held by his teammate, Larry Fitzgerald. DeAndre was 28 years old at that time.

OFF THE FIELD

DeAndre is a Christian and was baptized in 2012 while still at Clemson. In 2002, DeAndre's mother, Greenlee, lost her sight after a hot mixture of lye and bleach was thrown in her face by Savannah Grant, a lady who her boyfriend was having an affair with. Greenlee was rushed to the hospital and was in a three week long coma. She suffered burns on 17% of her body and, as a result, became blind.

Every game, she sits on the same seat, and after each touchdown DeAndre scores, he finds her and gives her the ball.

While DeAndre was at Clemson, he held a back-to-school giveaway of school supplies to children across America. He also partnered with the Feed A Million+ pledge to provide food to the needy.

CONCLUSION

Baseball may be America's leisure activity, but football has become America's favorite sport. Every year, more and more people participate in the sport, making it the most popular sport in the country. The regulations have altered over the years, sometimes for better and sometimes for worse. Even so, football has always maintained the mystique that led to it becoming the most popular sport in the USA. The NFL dominates Sunday television like no other event. Most supporters will tune in to any game, not just those involving their favorite team, making it a unique phenomenon among professional sports.

In 1920, the National Football League (NFL) was founded. Football is a hardcore sport, and we've seen some of history's best athletes on the gridiron proving it. Playing styles have come and gone over many decades. In the past, championships were won with a strong emphasis on defense and a ground game, but today, the passing game is king in the NFL. There have been gunslingers, precise passers, elusive yet powerful rushers, towering yet inaccessible slot receivers, and more. Given the wide variety of positions in the game and the wide range of possible skill sets, play styles, levels of athleticism, talent, and coaching, it is difficult to establish who the best player of all time is.

Arguments may be made for players like Tom Brady, Barry Sanders, Lawrence Taylor, and Jerry Rice, and all could be considered the best for different reasons. To identify the best player of all time, we must view not only their individual statistics and honors, the era in which they played the NFL, and the strengths and flaws of each player. The player's domination on the field and his impact on his team weighed heavily in my decision. I've discussed the 10 greatest players in the game's history from that perspective in this book. The players you read about in this book played during different eras and had very different styles. But, they are nonetheless the most incredible people to grace a football field.

Made in the USA
Middletown, DE
17 September 2023

38679213R00055